THE ASSESSMENT AND SELECTION HANDBOOK

THE ASSESSMENT AND SELECTION HANDBOOK

Tools, techniques and exercises for effective recruitment and development

Ian Taylor

KOGAN
PAGE

London and Philadelphia

Publisher's note
Every possible effort has been made to ensure that the information contained in this book is accurate at the time of going to press, and the publishers and author cannot accept responsibility for any errors or omissions, however caused. No responsibility for loss or damage occasioned to any person acting, or refraining from action, as a result of the material in this publication can be accepted by the editor, the publisher or the author.

First published entitled *A Practical Guide to Assessment Centres and Selection Methods* in Great Britain and the United States in 2007 by Kogan Page Limited

First published in paperback entitled *The Assessment and Selection Handbook* in 2008

Kogan Page Limited
120 Pentonville Road
London N1 9JN
United Kingdom
www.koganpage.com

Kogan Page US
525 South 4th Street, #241
Philadelphia PA 19147
USA

© Ian Taylor, 2008

ISBN 978 0 7494 5403 6

British Library Cataloguing-in-Publication Data

A CIP record for this book is available from the British Library.

Library of Congress Cataloging-in-Publication Data

Taylor, Ian, 1953–
  The assessment and selection handbook : tools, techniques and exercises for effective recruitment and development / Ian Taylor.
      p. cm.
  ISBN 978-0-7494-5403-6
1. Assessment centers (Personnel management procedure) 2. Employees--Rating of.
3. Employee selection. I. Title.
  HF5549.5.A78T37 2008
  658.3'112--dc22
                                    2008027144

Typeset by Saxon Graphics Ltd, Derby
Printed and bound in Great Britain by MPG Books Ltd, Bodmin, Cornwall

Contents

Acknowledgements   *viii*

Introduction   1

PART I. ASSESSMENT CENTRES

1. **Is Effective Selection Art or Science? The Case for Assessment Centres**   7
What are assessment centres? Two views 9; What are the differences between assessment and development centres? 11; How effective are assessment centres in comparison with other selection tools? 11; Why do assessment centres have higher validity? Seeing is believing 14; What are some of the issues associated with assessment centres? 17; 'Selling' the benefits of assessment centres 22; Key tips 26

2. **What Are We Assessing? Developing a Competence Framework**   27
What are competencies? 28; Types of competence 29; What competence frameworks are available? 30; Developing your own competence framework 31; What are some of the problems in using competence frameworks? 36; Sample framework 40; Key tips 46

3. Designing and Running an Assessment Centre   47
    What is the optimum time needed for assessment? 47; What to
    consider when using the activities 50; Communicating with
    participants 55; Evaluating the process 60; Key tips 62

4. Assessor Skills   63
    What makes a good assessor? 63; Remaining neutral – biases in
    assessment 64; Giving feedback 75; Where can I get assessors
    from? 81; Key tips 85

5. The Role of Psychometric Instruments in Assessment and
    Development   86
    What are psychometrics? 87; Should psychometrics be included as
    part of an assessment process? 90; What are some of the issues in
    using psychometrics? 94; Gaining access to psychometric tests 100;
    Key tips 102; Sample computer-generated psychometric reports 103

6. Adapting and Devising Activities   111
    Why devise your own activities? 111; Approaches to devising
    activities 112; Some additional activities 126; What if I am not so
    creative? 128; What's the future for assessments? 128; Key tips 129

7. Further Reading   130

PART II. ACTIVITIES

8. Role Plays   141
    Overview 141; Role play 1 142; Role play 2 146; Role play 3 149;
    Role play 4 152; Role play 5 155; Role play 6 158; Role play 7 164

9. In Trays   168
    Overview 168; In tray 1 170; In tray 2 172; In tray 3 174

10. Analytical/Report Writing Activities   178
    1 Crew scheduling 178; 2 Accommodation allocation 183; 3
    Transport manager 186

11. Open-ended Group Decision Making   192
    Overview 192; 1 Redundancy 193; 2 Delegation 197; 3 Charity
    allocation 202; 4 Selection centre 211

12. Physical Task Group Activities   215
    General introduction to group exercises in Chapters 12, 13
    and 14 215; 1 Construction tender 217; 2 Bridge building 221;
    3 River crossing 223

13. Mental Task Group Activities   225
    Overview 225; 1 Letter cards 226; 2 Cash register 228;
    3 Programme planning 235; 4 Broadcast appeal 240; 5 Who got
    the job? 242

14. Supplementary Group Activities   245
    Overview 245; 1 Committee on anti-social behaviour 246; 2 Paper
    castle 250; 3 Word groups 252; 4 Flight roster 255

    Index   *259*

Acknowledgements

The original concept for this book emerged from a number conversations with Hugh Fitz-Simons of Learning Curves. John Caunt made a significant number of suggestions and constructive criticisms which immeasurably improved the original format. I owe him a considerable debt for all the work he put into the project.

Carl Francis and Sabrina Braganza made valuable comments on early drafts of the book. Michael Mullen's computer skills saved me hours of frustration.

I have received personal support from a number of people: Charlotte Atyeo at Kogan Page; staff at The American Hospital, Dubai; Josie Gaspar; my son, Joseph, daughter Diosa and fiancée Amilyn Bitao. Thanks to all of you.

Introduction

This book is primarily a 'how to' manual. It provides the advice and tools for you to be able to easily and effectively introduce, design and deliver assessment or development centres in your organization. The focus throughout is *on assessing supervisory and first-line management* staff although the basic principles apply to all assessment centres.

The book has been created with busy HR and recruitment practitioners very much in mind. You may well have considered introducing assessment centres but, for a variety of reasons, have not so far been able to get the ball rolling.

You may have sensed, or directly experienced resistance to the idea from colleagues in line departments and perhaps were not sure how to convince them of the benefits. If so, Chapter 1 provides some practical tips for selling assessment centres to your colleagues.

Perhaps, on the other hand, you haven't been able to find the time in a hectic schedule to be able to sit down and design an entire process including a competence framework and exercises. Chapter 2 contains not only a sample framework, specifically designed for use at assessment centres, but also tips for sourcing or designing your own framework. You will also find in Chapter 2 a guide to help you decide which exercises to use to assess each competence.

Chapter 3 takes you through all the nitty gritty detail of running an assessment event, from pre-briefing to the organization of the actual event, ending with feedback and evaluation.

By now you may wonder how, even with a process in place, you will get the time to actually run assessment centres. Chapter 4 covers the practicalities of how to recruit and train a team of assessors to help you with the delivery of assessment centres. It covers the key skills required by assessors including recording evidence and debriefing activities.

Although you may know something about assessment centres, you may not feel sufficiently confident to debate the process with other people in your organization. To help you here, Chapter 1 contains a discussion of the key criteria used to guide the choice of selection tools in organizations and compares assessment centres with other commonly used methods. Chapter 5 focuses on one specific tool, psychometrics, and discusses its potential use in assessment and development.

The advice in the book is based throughout on contemporary research from occupational psychology. Chapter 7 contains suggestions for further reading which you can use to find out more about the theoretical issues which underpin the key messages in the book if you should wish to do so.

The cornerstone of the book is the activities in Chapters 8 to 14, which contain a number of practical, easy to use, exercises including:

* role plays;
* in trays;
* analytical/report writing exercises; and
* group problem-solving activities.

These activities are aimed at assessing *competencies commonly found at the supervisory and first-line manager level* and have been chosen with several criteria in mind:

* simple and easy to use with fairly short time-frames;
* require no expensive equipment;
* tried and tested.

The activities are set in a number of different contexts. You may find a slight leaning towards the aviation industry, reflecting the environment in which many of the exercises have been trialled. However, Chapter 6 provides you with guidance on how to easily tailor the activities to reflect different sectors or contexts. The activities are all reproduced in a .pdf format on the CD that accompanies this book, ready to print and use. If you need to amend them to meet your own specific requirements, please visit the publisher's website www.kogan-page.co.uk/ian_taylor for versions you can modify.

The international context

Many of the reports and best practice guidelines referred to in this book come from UK-based professional bodies such as the British Psychological Society and the Chartered Institute of Personnel and Development. However, the key messages apply to many other countries. To get a particular regional perspective please contact one of the appropriate bodies below.

HR representative bodies

World Federation of Personnel Management Associations: www.wfpma.com
Asia Pacific Federation of Human Resource Management: www.wfpma.org
North American Human Resource Management Association: www.shrm.org
European Association for Personnel Management: www.eapm.org
Hong Kong Institute of Human Resource Management: www.hkihrm.org

Representative bodies for psychologists

The Australian Psychological Society: www.psychology.org
American Psychological Association: www.apa.org
Canadian Psychological Association: www.cpa.ca
International Test Commission (ITC): www.intestcom.org

Part I
Assessment Centres

Is Effective Selection Art or Science? The Case for Assessment Centres

For the overstretched HR professional staff selection must, at times, feel like tiptoeing through a minefield. Have legal and ethical requirements been met? Can we be confident that the best person has been selected? Why do some line managers seem to treat the process so casually? What are the office politics around this appointment? Consider some typical situations.

Situation 1. Separating the lambs from the sheep

You've just run a series of interviews to select a new departmental manager. You received an extremely positive response from a number of highly qualified applicants. Shortlisting candidates was not a problem and some promising external candidates were invited to interview. The problems only started at the end of a long and tiring day.

It was seemingly impossible to differentiate between some well-prepared candidates. They all knew about the company background, gave plausible answers to why they wanted the job and were able to deliver textbook answers as to how they would tackle a conflict between two staff members.

Situation 2. Playing favourites?

You've completed a series of internal promotion interviews for a team leader role. The departmental head who interviewed with you is very keen to appoint one particular candidate. You are not so sure. The candidate seemed very nervous in the interview resulting in poor communication, was unclear about what strengths as a team leader she could bring to the role, preferring to concentrate on her years of experience in the department. She also came across as overly aggressive in her response to a hypothetical situation on dealing with an under-performance issue with a staff member.

In contrast you felt one candidate performed extremely well in the interview. She was articulate, gave appropriate answers to the under-performance issue and seemed well prepared about the challenges and opportunities a move to team leader would offer. The departmental manager, however, was adamant he did not want to appoint this candidate as she had a reputation for being pushy and aggressive in the workplace. When challenged the manager claimed he had only agreed to shortlist this candidate to avoid the conflict her early rejection would generate. Her performance appraisals were fine with no documented feedback about aggression.

You do not want to be sucked in to 'rubber-stamping' an appointment which you feel is unjustified. You think the line manager's motivation is based more on personal friendship and that he wants to appoint someone who will not challenge his approach or decisions.

Situation 3. Identifying top talent

Your organization has recently decided to introduce succession planning. You have been asked to prepare a report containing recommendations for selecting staff for a talent pool. This is a highly political issue and the process is bound to come under considerable scrutiny.

These are some fairly typical everyday situations faced by HR professionals. What approaches and tools are available to the busy HR professional to make objective decisions in these circumstances? Is it even possible to remain objective and scientific or must these types of decision remain, essentially, an art form?

Research indicates that there has been a steady rise in the use of assessment centres in the UK over the past 30 years. Forty-eight per cent of respondents to the CIPD's (Chartered Institute of Personnel and Development) 2006 Recruitment, Retention and Turnover Survey indicated that they used assessment centres 'to some degree'. This chapter aims to cover a lot of ground and provides:

- definitions of assessment centres;
- a comparison of assessment centres with other selection tools in terms of their ability to predict an individual's behaviour;
- reasons for the effectiveness of assessment centres as a selection and development tool;
- some of the more common criticisms of assessment centres and ways to counter these objections.

What are assessment centres? Two views

A 'technical' definition from occupational psychology

An assessment centre consists of a combination of selection tools. Typically, these activities include:

- *Work samples*, where small groups of participants undertake a series of activities under observation. The activities included in this book can all be looked at as work samples. These are role play meetings (Chapter 8), in tray activities (Chapter 9), analytical and report-writing activities (Chapter 10), group discussions (Chapter 11) and group tasks (Chapters 12, 13 and 14). Forty-eight per cent of respondents to the CIPD survey said that they used these tools 'in some way'.

- *Simulations*. These are more typically used for more senior appointments or in development centres. They often involve participants taking on a senior role in a fictitious company and completing a range of tasks related to their role. They usually require a longer time-frame than a series of work sample activities.

- *Interviews*. Although different forms of interview are identified in the 2006 CIPD survey, in general the interview remains by far the most commonly used selection tool. Interviews were described as being used in some way by 81 to 88 per cent of respondents depending on the type of interview.

- *Psychometrics*. Personality tests were used, 'in some way', by 60 per cent of respondents to the CIPD survey, specific tests of ability by 82 per cent and general ability tests by 75 per cent. Chapter 5 looks in detail at the use of psychometrics in selection and assessment.

A 'lay' definition often used informally in organizations

This is more limited in scope and generally refers only to the use of a number of work samples. Often in organizations when the phrase 'assessment centre' is used it is, in reality, only a section of a longer process that is being referred to.

What are the differences between assessment and development centres?

In essence the processes may look fairly similar and use the same exercises. Assessment centres are designed primarily for selection whereas development centres identify potential and training needs. The key difference comes in the management of the process. Development centres may use more extensive debriefs and give participants feedback as the process continues. They are not pass/fail events. The output is most usually a formal, written, feedback report and associated development plan. Chapter 4 explores these issues in more depth. This means that development centres are often more resource-intensive than assessment centres.

Succession planning is one key area in which development centres are used. The CIPD claims that:

> in a climate of growing skills shortages and lack of confidence in the leadership potential of the existing workforce, interest in succession planning has revived. But the new succession planning looks quite different from the old version, with a broader vision and far closer links to wider talent management practices. (CIPD Fact Sheet, 2006)

Succession planning is usually reserved for more senior roles. However, development centres are being increasingly used to assess current and future potential in more junior roles. This might be where a line manager asks for assistance in gaining a more objective and detached opinion about a particular team member. The resulting information is most usually used to produce a focused and appropriate development plan.

How effective are assessment centres in comparison with other selection tools?

Time for some jargon! Occupational psychologists use a number of criteria to evaluate the effectiveness of selection tools.

Any measurement tool can be evaluated in terms of its *validity*. For selection tools we are really interested in *criterion validity*. In the organizational context we primarily want to know how effective a tool is in predicting an individual's ability in a particular work-related competence, although other work-related criteria such as length of time in a job (tenure) or ability to complete a training course can also be used. Sometimes this is also known as *predictive validity*.

Two other aspects of validity which will be discussed later in this chapter, and also in Chapter 5 on psychometrics, include construct and content validity.

Construct validity asks if the tool actually measures the characteristic it has been designed to assess, or something else. For example, a criticism of role plays is that they really measure acting ability rather than real skill. In another context some would suggest a 'closed book' formal examination measures memory or ability to work under pressure rather than knowledge or intelligence. For some selection tools, such as work samples, construct and criterion validity are virtually the same in that they measure ability in a particular competence. For other tools, however, they can be quite different, for example in a personality test where construct validity refers to an aspect of personality, say extroversion. This distinction is important in explaining the effectiveness of different instruments, as we will see later.

Content validity asks if the tool tests the whole range of characteristics in the domain. For example, does an activity such as a role play measure all the defined aspects of a competence such as 'Customer Service' including questioning, empathy and considering the needs of different groups, or does it really only measure empathy? Similarly, does a personality test measuring extroversion include all the various aspects of the construct such as warmth, openness, social boldness and group orientation?

The most compelling evidence regarding the criterion validity of selection tools comes from various meta-analyses. A meta-analysis is the combined result of a large number of research studies. Individual studies are argued to be less accurate because of their:

- Small sample sizes.

- Restricted sample range. It is usually only successful candidates whose performance can be measured. There is no way to track non-selected candidates or know how they would have performed in a particular role.

- Unreliability of criterion measures. For example, is it safe to assume that all managers' ratings of their team's performance ratings are totally objective and reliable indicators of performance?

Validity statistics provide a correlation coefficient which can range from 1, where, in simple terms we might say the tool provides perfect prediction, to 0, indicating no correlation or predictability. So how do assessment centres measure up in terms of criterion validity?

If we take the technical definition of a combination of tools, validity from different studies ranges from as high as 0.7, extremely good, to 0.4, moderate. The lower ratings can be explained by the difficulties in combining the sometimes contradictory evidence a range of tools can produce. Using the more informal definition of a series of work samples, the validity of assessment centres is consistently rated as 'good'.

Table 1.1 Criterion validity for some selection tools

Validity	Tools
Good (0.5 and above)	Work samples Ability tests Structured interview (either based on CV or behavioural competence)
Moderate (0.30 – 0.49)	Some objective methods of filtering paper applications, for example bio data, training and experience evaluations, weighted applications blanks Conscientiousness
Low/Nil (0.29 or below)	Unstructured interviews Interests/hobbies Education Personality inventories (except conscientiousness) Graphology (analysis of handwriting)

Why do assessment centres have higher validity? Seeing is believing

'Recruit for attitude, train for skill' runs the cliché. But is this necessarily the case and is it practical to do this? Think about some of the more celebrated and frequently used selection tools: an audition for actors and other performers, a simulator check in pilot recruitment, a presentation for a sales executive, a test of PC office applications for a secretary. In discussing internal applicants, selectors frequently comment that in comparison to external applicants at least it is 'the devil we know'.

Many organizations are now attempting to get the entire workforce to think of themselves as recruiters by getting staff to encourage skilled people they know to be effective to apply to the company. Some companies ask new recruits to recommend three people to approach from their old organization. They can even go as far as targeting conferences to recruit the high-performing sales staff of their rivals!

What do these seemingly diverse approaches have in common? They are based on an assessment of behaviour. In effective selection we are attempting to extract information about the candidate's *behaviour*. That is verbal behaviour, everything a person says, and visual behaviour, everything they do.

At work it is behaviour that produces results, if it's appropriate, or causes problems, if it's inappropriate. At work, behaviour is observable. We see people taking an interest in a customer as well as hearing them ask, for instance, an open question. We hear a manager raising his or her voice to a member of staff and see him or her waving a finger at them. We also see the results of these behaviours.

It is behaviour that produces a response from others, whether that response is a smile, agreement, a counter-argument, a proposal or whatever. Behaviour is something that we exercise control over and something that we can modify and adapt to fit the situation. We behave in a way that can help us achieve a positive result in a situation or, if we choose the wrong behaviour, no result at all.

The problem with tools such as the interview is that we only observe a very narrow range of behaviours in an artificial situation. As we can adapt our behaviour, people are likely to behave differently in an interview. There are different pressures and unclear expectations of how to behave at the interview. Therefore, some candidates may go for the quiet unassuming approach even if they are quite determined and forceful at work. Others behave in an overly confident way at interview, which does not necessarily reflect their style of dealing with people in work settings.

What many interviews settle for is trying to interpret the internal state of the candidate. Internal states include:

- *Values.* Values represent our ideals, relatively permanent ideas about what we feel *should* be. These are based in experiences, people, concepts or institutions that we hold dear. When a selector makes a comment like, 'She appears to feel most at home in a company that gives her freedom to develop her ideas' he or she is inferring the candidate's values.

- *Beliefs.* These are opinions or judgements that fall short of certainty. A selector commenting on beliefs may say something like, 'He seems to think that the best way to manage people is by involving them in the decisions made about their work'.

- *Feelings.* Emotional reactions that influence how the person deals with a situation. 'She seems to get angry/upset/pleased/hurt when she is left alone to do a job by her superiors', would be an example of making inferences about a candidate's feelings about a situation.

- *Motives.* These are goals that drive behaviour. Needs like, 'the need to belong', 'the need to feel secure', 'the need to be liked' are examples of motivational goals. An interviewer commenting on a candidate's motivation will use phrases like, 'He needs to feel that he is an important part of the team' or, 'She needs recognition'.

These internal state factors have two things in common. We can't see them, we can only suspect or, at best, make inferences about them. They are also fairly rigid and unchangeable. Changes to values and beliefs take a long time.

The other major internal state that traditional interviewers attempt to explore is a candidate's *personality*. Again this cannot be observed directly and assessments are often based on flimsy evidence. Personality tends to be fixed from a fairly early age. Personality changes, when they do occur, are normally a 'traumatic' experience rather then a gradual process over time.

Typical comments about a candidate's *personality* include:

'She is an extrovert.'
'He is quite shy.'
'She is lazy.'
'He is an introvert.'
'She has a likeable personality.'
'He has a sense of humour.'
'She is very confident.'
'She is a self-motivated person.'
'He is impatient.'

So what is wrong with comments on the candidate's internal state? Surely it's as critical to success in the job as behaviour? At first sight that appears a convincing argument. Personality and attitudes can affect behaviour, although the degree to which this occurs is the subject of some debate amongst psychologists. A number of studies such as Azjen and Fishbein (1977; see Chapter 7 for full details), have shown that attitudes are, contrary to popular opinion, not necessarily good predictors of behaviour. In reality, when many recruiters talk about attitudes they are using broad concepts, a 'positive attitude to change', rather than a specific attitude to, say, a particular reorganization. These broader concepts not only show poor links to behaviour but also run the risk of encouraging recruiters to become overly judgmental.

Behaviour is something that we can choose and change to fit the situation we are in. So our personality and attitudes are only indicators, and fairly imprecise ones, of how we may behave in certain situations. For instance, I can feel very angry about something my boss does to me but I can choose whether to 'blow my top' and shout at her, or remain calm and placid. She could infer from the latter behaviour that I am a quiet and placid person. If underneath that behaviour I am very angry and feel aggressive, her inference is clearly wrong. If, on the other hand, she were to concentrate on my behaviour and conclude that most of the time I behaved in a fairly calm way, she would have hard evidence for this statement. If I chose to 'blow my top' then she could conclude that at times I raised my voice. If she were then able to pinpoint what triggered this behaviour she could choose whether or not to risk using this trigger in future. In this example my 'internal state' is not an issue. The only important factor is my behaviour, what I say and do and the situation that triggers that behaviour.

In essence then, the selection tools with the highest criterion validity, competence-based interviews, ability tests and work samples, have been designed with the specific purpose of measuring particular competencies. Construct and criterion validity can then be considered to be close or identical in what they are measuring. Methods with lower validity have been designed to measure something else, for example personality, from which another criterion can be inferred. Construct and criterion validity in these cases measure different things. Maybe it would be more helpful to say 'recruit for core skill, then train for company processes and procedures'?

What are some of the issues associated with assessment centres?

Reliability

This refers to consistency of measurement. Would different assessors come to the same rating decision using the same evidence? An ability test marked by using a scoring template or a computer with only one correct answer per question can be said to have high reliability. However, assessing performance in, say, a role play is not quite so straightforward. The process is much more open to individual interpretation. In Chapter 4 a number of ways to improve 'inter-rater reliability' are outlined.

Face validity of activities

Face validity describes the appearance, to the person being tested, that a test measures what it is claiming to measure. For example, a group activity asking participants to build a bridge from paper may have low face validity. 'What's this got to do with real life?' may run the objection. On the other hand, asking a candidate to run a performance appraisal in a role play or make a sales presentation may be seen to have much greater direct relevance to the job in question. Similarly, a statement from a personality test such as, 'I usually enjoy spending time talking to friends about social events or parties' will have much higher face validity than a statement such as, 'I prefer a shower to a bath'. This is important mainly in PR terms. If a selection tool is perceived, for whatever reason, to be irrelevant then this may restrict the number of applicants for posts.

In the UK the Chief Constable of the Thames Valley Police Force made a public criticism of a Home Office promotion examination consisting of role plays to demonstrate leadership and problem solving. He called the process 'absurd' stating that:

> I have good officers that I would promote tomorrow but they have failed the role play exam or else are not prepared to subject themselves to it... to insist on a test that is no indicator of the competence of an officer is the politics of the madhouse.

In essence, the Chief Constable was criticizing the face validity of this process.

Fairness

Adverse impact occurs if a selection tool is discriminatory, in other words if it favours one group over another, for example a sex, race or cultural group. Most statistical adverse impact studies have been conducted on ability tests. The British Psychological Society (BPS) guidelines for best practice in assessment centres suggest that:

differential performance or scores associated with membership of a particular ethnic, gender or other group should always be investigated further. If this does not reflect real differences in performance potential on the job, it could well lead to illegal *indirect discrimination* under the law'. (*Design, Implementation and Evaluation of Assessment and Development Centres; Best practice guidelines*, British Psychological Society, available from the Psychological Testing Centre)

Indeed, a recent CIPD report (*Diversity in Business. How much progress have employers made? First findings*) argues that managing diversity 'involves a more proactive and inclusive agenda than minimal compliance with equal opportunities legislation'. The report goes on to state that whilst legal pressures were by far the top driver for managing diversity there are also considerable business benefits for diversity, such as recruiting and retaining the best talent.

The activities in this book, indeed like most commercially available work sample activities, have not been subjected to any adverse impact studies. It is therefore important that you track the performance of different groups in the various activities to monitor for bias.

Utility

Most organizations are cost conscious! It is important, therefore, to be able to show that the benefits of using a particular selection method outweigh the costs. Occupational psychologists have developed a technique called *utility analysis* to evaluate the financial benefits of assessment centres. The results of this technique have provided two general rules of thumb. These are, first, that the difference between the good and average performer in terms of value is between 40 to 70 per cent of salary and, secondly, that the good performer is twice as productive as the poor performer.

The resulting logic, if we accept the higher validity of some selection tools presented above, is that there is a strong basis for justifying the extra resources involved in assessment centres in terms of the cost savings of selecting higher performers.

The 2006 CIPD Recruitment, Retention and Turnover Survey estimated the costs of recruitment for a managerial/professional employee to be £5,000 or just under US $10,000, made up of advertising and search fees. In addition, labour turnover costs were estimated at £12,500 or around US $24,500 in terms of vacancy cover, recruitment, training and induction. In the context of these figures the costs of assessment centres can therefore also be seen to be relatively small.

Cultural issues

There are some links here to the earlier point on fairness. The question is, do the techniques apply worldwide? This can emerge in a number of ways. Does the competence framework used reflect different cultural approaches to management, a theme explored in more depth in Chapter 2? For example, a direct, open approach to conflict resolution is not always seen as appropriate in all countries and cultures. Some cultures emphasize a more indirect approach. Pilot recruitment in many airlines now looks to assess so-called 'soft skills' such as assertiveness and consensual decision making. These skills may not naturally fit into some cultures that stress deference to authority. However, in the context of aviation safety there is a wealth of well documented evidence that passive or overly aggressive pilots can compromise safety.

We might also ask if the exercises fit into the cultural background of the participants. For example, assigned role discussion group activities, such as activity 3, 'Charity Allocation', in Chapter 11, may discriminate against those whose culture does not emphasize an overtly competitive approach as each participant has to argue a specific case in competition with other participants. Of course, in these circumstances, the activity can always be modified by removing the assigned roles and making the exercise more of a group consensus discussion. To take another example, an activity such as number 1 'Committee on Anti-social Behaviour' in Chapter 14 may not be appropriate in, say, a situation where most participants are Muslim, as the discussion centres around ways to reduce alcohol consumption. However, it could be argued that this does not preclude participants being able to make a considered decision about the effectiveness of a particular suggestion based on their 'Analytical Thinking' skills.

How 'public' is the process?

In the 'information age', vast amounts of information, both authorized and unauthorized, are available about companies through simple internet searches. This includes information about what the company is like to work for and how it runs its selection processes. If a centre is used regularly, particularly as part of mass recruitment, then the process runs the risk of becoming 'contaminated' as the activities become widely available in the public domain. Two pilot-based websites serve to illustrate the point: www.pprune.org, a 'pilot rumour network' and www.willflyforfood.cc, described as a 'pilot interview gouge site'. These sites provide detailed descriptions of pilot selection procedures at a wide range of airlines. Similarly, some enterprising former cabin crew offer courses preparing would-be applicants for specific airline selection procedures.

It can, therefore, often appear that the candidates know more about the process than the selectors! Over-prepared candidates can in fact, at times, harm rather than help their chances. In the group activities, for example, it is tempting for some candidates to feel that if they can provide the best solutions to the specific task or problem then they will score well in the various competencies. This, however, is not necessarily the case. It is generally group process competencies such as 'Interpersonal Skill' or 'Influencing' that are being assessed rather than the accuracy of a partic-ular solution.

Online assessments

Chapter 5 discusses the increasing use of online administration in psychometric testing. Although still relatively rare in practice, some work sample activities can be administered online. This issue is discussed in more depth in Chapter 6. Of the activities contained in this book those in Chapters 9 (In Trays) and 10 (Analytical/Report Writing) could be administered unsupervised online or in a supervised environment directly on to computers. Although this can be highly cost-effective there are some obvious implications in terms of security and cheating.

'Selling' the benefits of assessment centres

The bad news is that in the 2005 CIPD Recruitment, Retention and Turnover Survey the top three most effective selection methods identified by employees were, exclusively, some form of an interview. Although they may not talk in technical terms of face validity or reliability, these issues typically emerge in everyday objections to the use of assessment centres:

> 'Stupid games with no relevance to real life.'
> 'Too costly.'
> 'I don't need this psychobabble. With 20-plus years experience I can tell who can do the job after a five-minute chat.'
> 'Good idea but where am I going to get the time from?'
> 'It's all about your ability to act, not about real skill.'

So what might be some appropriate responses to these objections?

Not relevant

The exercises in Chapters 12, 13 and 14, often those most subject to accusations of being irrelevant, are designed to gain evidence of the following behaviours and abilities in *non-standard, unusual, neutral context* situations:

- manage multiple tasks;
- use a range of decision-making styles as appropriate (directive to participative);
- see the 'big picture' and identify critical information;

- communicate effectively;
- use resources to accomplish a task;
- work under time pressure.

The use of non-standard, non-work-based situations is critical. This enables you to assess candidates with a wide range of backgrounds at the same time. The activities in the book are not designed to test knowledge of company rules and procedures as applied in routine situations, but rather to assess candidates' approach to less standardized situations.

Using activities based on specific work situations runs a number of risks. Candidates with no specific knowledge of the particular operation can, justifiably, claim to be disadvantaged. On the other hand, candidates with detailed knowledge of the operation can get sidetracked into questioning the accuracy of the brief. At times then, despite issues of face validity, it is often more effective to set tasks in a completely neutral context.

Attribution theory, which is covered in more detail in Chapter 4, is an attempt to explain how different people explain events. In simple terms it suggests that most people have a tendency to explain negative events, such as failure to be selected for a job, in terms of the situation, 'The assessment was all about playing stupid games, what's that got to do with work?' rather than in terms of personal attributes. So, although you may not want to refer to psychological theories when trying to sell assessment centres, it can be reassuring to know that accusations of lack of relevance are not only common but normal, and even healthy!

Costs

The data on the utility of selection methods can help to counter objections of costs. The costs of recruitment and the hidden cost of hiring the wrong person far outweigh the additional costs of using a wider range of selection tools, particularly if in-house resources are used. Of course there are also hidden costs in using assessment centres, notably the costs of training and utilizing a team of non-specialist assessors. However, this experience can provide other benefits, outlined in Chapter 4, in terms of increased skill and motivation.

Validity

The data presented above in the section on 'utility' provides compelling evidence that work samples, the key element in the lay definition of assessment centres, provide the strongest validity in comparison to all other selection tools.

Acting

If candidates can act through an assessment exercise such as a group activity or role play this surely indicates that they not only know what is required but can also display the appropriate behaviours. However, what we are not sure of is if they will continue to display these behaviours on a regular, consistent, basis. This is something that most work samples are not really designed to assess so, in essence, it is unfair to criticize a process for something it has not been set up to measure, although this will probably not stop people continuing to do so!

Indeed, many jobs require 'emotional labour'. Emotional labour has been described as 'the management of feeling to create a publicly observable facial and bodily display' or, 'the effort, planning and control needed to express organizationally desired emotion'. So, in addition to physical and intellectual labour, sections of the workforce, it has been suggested, are paid to also express prescribed emotions, or in other words, to act!

These emotions are defined through display and feelings rules. Display rules tend to be more specific and are often made explicit in training manuals or job instructions. Examples include phrases such as 'friendliness, displayed empathy' from a call centre operator appraisal form and, 'passengers shall receive a friendly welcome... and will be bid farewell cheerfully' from an airline job instruction manual. Feeling rules, on the other hand, are less precisely defined than display rules and are embedded in the organizational culture. Frequently organizational mission statements or core values encourage the expression of particular emotions. Examples taken from *101 Great Mission Statements* by Timothy Foster (Kogan Page) include 'An environment that rewards achievement, enthusiasm and team spirit' (DHL Worldwide) and 'Enjoy your work and always brighten your working atmosphere' (Honda).

A wide range of roles can therefore be seen as requiring emotional labour and have been the subject of research studies. The more obvious examples are of front-line customer service roles such as flight attendants, hairdressers, fast-food counter servers, sales people, bank clerks and supermarket cashiers. Some take an even broader view, suggesting that if we include feeling rules there are few roles that do not require some form of emotional labour or, in essence, acting! Emotional labour researchers are interested in the degree to which employees engage in either deep acting, trying to actually summon the required emotions, or surface acting defined as just 'going through the motions'.

Assessment centres provide a legally defensible selection system

The objective, recorded assessments of the assessment centre can prove invaluable in the event of legal challenges to selection decisions, which are on the rise in many areas.

Well organized and run assessment centres can actually impress candidates

For external candidates who are also, in many cases, potential customers, the recruitment process can be the first direct contact they have with the organization. The assessment process presents a valuable opportunity to establish the overall brand of the organization. Giving feedback to candidates can further enhance this image, even though there are resource, and in extreme cases legal, implications to this.

Resistors to change

Influencing strategies can be divided into *push,* also called 'solution-based' and *pull* or 'problem-based'. Pull strategies tend to generate more long-term commitment and agreement because they involve all stakeholders in producing a joint solution to a commonly agreed problem. Push strategies can, where there is no formal power or authority, be less effective and generate more resistance. Unfortunately, when selling assessment centres to other colleagues you will usually, by definition, be using a push strategy as you already have the 'best' solution in mind. It is, therefore, important that you have a range of arguments in place to back up your position unless you are in the rare position of a colleague approaching you asking for ways to improve a selection process.

Whichever argument you use it is important to recognize that many objections to change are, in essence, driven by an emotional reaction. For many, change is stressful: it takes us out of our comfort zone. In these cases using objective, rational, arguments is unlikely to get you very far as an influencing strategy. The key is to work out if the stated objection communicates the real issue or is a mask for a more fundamental, emotional, resistance.

Although not easy to do, try to identify those colleagues you feel may be, at least, amenable to some rational arguments and have an open mind to change.

Key tips

- Work samples are one of the most effective selection tools in terms of their ability to predict future performance. Include these in your assessment centres if they are relevant to the role being assessed.

- Think about how you might sell the concept of assessment centres to key stakeholders. Initially start with those you feel are basically open to persuasion. Try to match your argument to the objection.

- Assessment centres are not always the most appropriate selection tool. Junior or temporary jobs may not warrant the extra resources required, so evaluate whether using an assessment centre is right for every selection.

2

What Are We Assessing? Developing a Competence Framework

By this stage you have, hopefully, been convinced that assessment centres would add value to your selection processes. This still leaves the nitty gritty issues of how to go about designing and running an assessment centre.

The first, and one of the most critical building blocks in the design of an assessment or development centre is to decide what exactly it is you want to assess and then to what standard or level. The mechanism most frequently used to address this issue is a *competence framework*. This chapter looks at how competencies have been defined, where to find an appropriate competence framework and then how to decide which framework best meets your needs. The chapter ends with a sample framework designed for use with the exercises in the book and gives recommendations of which activities to use in assessing each competence.

What are competencies?

The UK's CIPD describes competencies as:

> a signal from the organization to the individual of the expected areas and levels of performance. They provide the individual with a map or indication of the behaviours that will be valued, recognized and in some organizations rewarded. Competencies can be understood to represent the language of performance in an organization, articulating both the expected outcomes of an individual's efforts and the manner in which these activities are carried out.

Competence has been defined in different ways. Some see competence as an underlying characteristic of an individual that causally relates to superior performance in a job or situation. This is a fairly wide definition and includes aspects such as:

- *motives*, for example the motivation to achieve;
- *traits and attitudes* such as conscientiousness;
- *self-concept*, say the level of self-confidence;
- *knowledge*;
- *behaviours or skills.*

Others see competence more narrowly, in terms of a set of observable behaviours. In essence, competencies are defined only in terms of skills. As we saw in Chapter 1, they argue that the causes of behaviour are not only difficult to measure but are, in a sense, irrelevant in that we only really need to know if people can display certain behaviours, not why.

Whilst it can be highly beneficial to find out what motivates prospective employees, it is also very difficult to do in practice. Motives are internal to the person. In general we infer them through what people do or say; in other words; their behaviours. This leads us back into assessing only behaviours. There are some questionnaires that aim to assess motives, values or attitudes. However, as discussed in Chapter 1, these have high face validity, so in the 'high stakes' situation of a job selection, it is relatively easy for the candidate to provide those answers they feel are required and are more acceptable to the selectors, rather than those that reflect their true feelings. For these reasons the activities in this book have been designed to measure and assess only behaviours, not traits or motives.

Types of competence

Universals

These are competencies that could be seen to be related to performance in just about any job. From the sample framework, examples would be 'Interpersonal Skill' and 'Oral Communication'.

Occupationals

These are competencies that relate to a specific job or family of jobs. For example, an accountant would need to be particularly competent in numerical reasoning. In the sample framework, 'Leadership' might be an example of an 'occupational' in that it does not apply to the vast majority of jobs. 'Customer Service' is an interesting example in that in the past it might have been seen as an occupational relating only to front-line service delivery roles. Increasingly, however, with the growth in the concept of the internal customer, we might see 'Customer Service' as a universal suggesting that the distinction between different types of competence is not always clear cut.

Relationals

What is required in a particular job can vary widely according to the particular setting of the job. For example, a lawyer working in a small local law centre may well face different challenges to a lawyer working in a large city practice. So the competence of 'Independence' might be more appropriate for this situation. A pilot working in a multicultural environment may require additional skills than a pilot who works for an airline that primarily recruits cockpit crew from one country. Some organizations may therefore include a competence of 'cross-cultural understanding'.

Sometimes these qualities are characterized as 'fit', so the issue becomes how do we select for fit, or for the person being happy at work? This sense of fit can be influenced by a number of factors, including how the individual's values relate to a sense of achievement, work/life balance and opportunities for growth in the organizational culture. Obviously, despite the examples given above, these cannot always be easily reduced to a behavioural competence framework. For that reason, and also because they are individual to specific organizations, these have not been included in the sample framework. Usually these are more appropriately assessed in a structured interview. It is also possible to use values questionnaires, but in 'high stakes' situations such as job selection, candidates may well fake their responses to provide the profile they feel is required by the organization (see Chapter 5).

What competence frameworks are available?

Competence frameworks are available from a number of sources.

You may be working in an organization that already uses a competence framework as part of its approach to performance management. A recent benchmarking study (Rankin, 2004) found that 76 per cent of organizations surveyed used, or were about to introduce, a competence framework.

There are also publicly available frameworks, a good example of which is provided by the MSC (Management Standards Centre; www.management-standards.org.uk). The MSC is the UK government-recognized standards setting body for the management and leadership areas. The MSC has been engaged in a publicly funded project to develop a new set of National Occupational Standards (NOS) for management and leadership. The new standards, which were approved in May 2004, describe the level of performance expected in employment for a range of management and leadership functions/activities.

The standards are organized into six functional areas which are then sub-divided into a number of units. The six areas are: Managing Self and Personal Skills, Providing Direction, Facilitating Change, Working with People, Using Resources and Achieving Results. Each unit contains a range of 'generic skills', which equate most closely to the behaviours the activities in the pack are designed to assess. If you are working with the MSC 1997 standards the activities in this book are the broad equivalent of the 'personal competencies' at levels three and four.

A rigorous search of the internet will unearth a number of other frameworks. For frameworks available in other countries, contact one of the HR representative bodies listed in the introduction. Many occupational psychology consultancies that sell assessment centre activities also provide competence frameworks. Whilst they may include a list of competencies in their promotional material these rarely include behaviour indicators. These are usually only available once materials have been purchased.

A sample framework for use with the practical activities is provided at the end of this chapter. Alternatively, you may want to develop your own framework from scratch or to adapt an existing framework. Several methods are available to help in the systematic development of a competence framework. Two of the most commonly used methods, critical incident analysis and repertory grid analysis, are described here. When using either method you should consult as wide a range of people as possible, including job-holders and relevant managers.

Developing your own competence framework

Critical incident analysis

It's frequently said that airline pilots get paid 99 per cent of their salary for 1 per cent of the job: the key incidents when they can make the difference between a disaster and a safe outcome. Although the 'critical incidents' in many other jobs may not have quite the same dramatic impact they are still the situations that go to make a real difference in the individual's effectiveness, for example when a sales assistant handles a customer complaint or unusual request.

Use these key steps to conduct a simple critical incident analysis:

1. List the key demands. The key demands of a job are the things that *must* be done. They are the two or three things which, if staff get them right, can really make a difference. Demands will come from a variety of sources such as the boss, customers, colleagues or other staff. They are often unstated expectations and can conflict with each other. For example, the boss wants you to follow procedures whilst the customer wants you to be flexible.

2. Analyse the constraints in the job. These are the 'grit in the works', the things that make the demands difficult to meet. They can be real, such as rules and regulations, or assumed and imagined, for example, 'I can't challenge my boss'. Conflicting demands can also feel like constraints.

3. List job tasks. Note down all the tasks the job holder carried out in the past five days. Add other tasks to give a true reflection of the job if the past five days are not 'typical'.

4. Define each task in terms of difficulty, importance and frequency. Difficulty is obviously subjective and hard to pin down. It will depend on experience and ability, to a degree. Refer back to step 2 which may help to define difficult tasks. Importance is also difficult to define. To some extent all tasks can be important, or difficult to class as unimportant. Therefore, some comparison is appropriate, ranking tasks against other tasks. Factors to consider when judging importance are:
   – cost implications if things go wrong;
   – numbers of people potentially affected by a decision;
   – whether a decision has internal or external implications;
   – source of the request: from a senior manager or a junior manager?

An example might be of an airline check-in agent. The routine part of the job such as processing passenger tickets would be 'frequent' but hopefully not too difficult after training and some experience. However, the element of the job that might be difficult and important would be handling irate passengers. This is where the agent could really make a significant difference in the skill of handling the complaint. It is also an area where there may be conflicting demands.

5. Identify critical incidents. These will become apparent by looking at tasks that are both very difficult and very important. They can also be defined by thinking about situations which involve conflicting demands and constraints.

6. Identify key competencies. What skills and abilities are needed to handle the critical incidents effectively? To take the airline check-in agent example, this could be either interpersonal ability or customer service.

7. Agree behaviour indicators. For each competence we need to ask what specifically a person does when they do this well, or poorly. At this stage it is helpful to identify actual good and poor performers then ask what it is they specifically do that differentiates them. This provides us with our behaviour indicators and makes sure all assessors are working from the same viewpoint. For some competencies it may be that different people have different views of what constitutes a skilled approach. For example, effective leadership, if left as a broad heading such as 'the ability to lead a team', can be looked at in many different ways.

Writing behaviour indicators

Behaviour indicators are a vital element in the construction of effective competencies. Well-constructed behaviour indicators lessen the potential effects of the 'exercise effect' (see Chapter 3) and also aid the feedback process.

Effective behaviour indicators, as much as possible, need to be:

- Specific not vague/subjective. 'Effective', 'relevant style', 'resilient', 'creative and innovative' are all too vague to be helpful. To take the example of 'Creativity', in the sample framework presented at the end of this chapter two behaviour indicators are suggested: 'Challenges constraints by looking for different interpretations' and 'Suggests novel or unusual solutions and approaches'. Whilst these still require an element of interpretation they are more precise than 'creative'.

- Based on one behaviour, not two or more ('fluent and effective', 'able to identify the main objective and maintain focus', 'energetic and proactive', 'concise and relevant', 'cooperates and consults'). This is not always feasible without producing a seemingly endless list of behaviours. At some point, however, we need to assume that a skilled assessor is aware of the various component parts of, say, 'generating rapport/empathy by use of appropriate body language and voice tone' under 'Customer Service'. To produce too long a list runs the possibility of introducing the exercise effect, explained in detail in Chapter 3.

- Observed internal states ('reminds group of time') not inferred ('conscious of time-frame', 'views problems as challenges', 'encourages two-way communication').

- Neutral ('exceeds time allocated') not based on values/judgmental ('articulate').

- Realistic ('regularly', 'appropriately') not impossible ('fully involved in all aspects and throughout').

- Written in straightforward 'jargon-free' terms. For example, 'backs up suggestions with reasons' rather than 'able to demonstrate rationale behind an assertion or suggestion'.

- Appropriate to behaviours typically shown in the activities.

Negative (or less effective) behaviours are more than simply not displaying the positive and it is essential that they are also clearly identified. They can include:

- failure to demonstrate a positive behaviour, or enough quality and quantity of the positive indicator;
- demonstrating the complete opposite of a positive behaviour ('builds on others' ideas by asking questions' with 'interrupts others');
- overdoing a positive behaviour to the point where it becomes a liability ('constantly gives feedback');
- inappropriate use of a positive behaviour. In other words, the right behaviour but at the wrong time or situation, for example trying to get consensus when there is little available time and a quick decision needs to be made.

Repertory grid analysis ('rep grid')

Rep grid analysis is based on personal construct theory originally developed by psychologist George Kelly for use in clinical settings. The technique is used for an individual to make explicit his or her internal constructs. A construct is a mechanism we use to help make sense of situations. For example, we might want to find out what constructs people use to define what for them is a 'good manager'. Rather than giving them a pre-determined list to choose from, rep grid analysis allows participants in the process to identify their own criteria or constructs.

Rep grid analysis can be quite a complex process. To help you, use either a specialist book such as Fransella *et al* (2003), or an occupational psychologist, preferably chartered with the BPS in the UK or registered with one of the representative professional bodies for psychologists in other countries (see the Introduction for a full list). They might be working independently or for a larger consultancy.

In essence, and taking the earlier example of a 'good manager', the technique requires each participant to write down the names of six managers they have worked with, two who they felt were excellent, two poor and two moderate or midway between the extremes. They would then go on to compare the six in groups of three and, thinking in behavioural terms only, identify what distinguishes one of the three from the other two (two 'meet staff in their own working area', one 'sees staff in his office'). As various groupings of three are constructed the process continues until a number of contrasts emerge. Finally, the six managers would be rated, one to six on the grid, according to how like the description of each pair they are and then correlated with the effectiveness rating of each as a manager.

What are some of the problems in using competence frameworks?

They do not provide clear cut, black and white standards

It is best to think of a competence framework in terms of a broad mental road map to guide your thinking rather than a set of rigid standards. There is obviously a considerable degree of subjectivity in terms of interpreting phrases such as 'speaks quickly'. The phrase 'appropriately' appears frequently in the sample framework and this assumes a certain degree of prior knowledge. As you will see in Chapter 4, this element of interpretation is one of the greatest challenges facing any team of assessors.

As you can also see in any framework there is often overlap between different competencies. In the sample framework, for example, 'Customer Service' and 'Interpersonal Skill' have considerable overlap, and it is not always possible to rigidly specify where one begins and another ends. If a participant suggests an initial plan, is that recorded under 'Initiative' or 'Planning and Organizing' if both competencies are being assessed? At times a positive behaviour in one competence could equally be argued to be a less effective behaviour in another. At what point does 'acts decisively' from 'Leadership' become 'blocks proposals' under 'Interpersonal Skill'?

Overall it is not helpful to think of competencies as completely objective standards in the same way as, say, a multiple-choice test with one, and only one, correct answer for each question. Trying to establish this degree of objectivity is likely to cause you more problems than it solves!

As suggested earlier, it is easier to think of competencies in terms of a broad guideline.

Are we assessing what actually is, or what we would like to be?

An interesting issue surrounding the use of competencies is the extent to which they reflect the actual reality of life in organizations. It may well be good management practice to act assertively in conflict situations or to carefully plan ahead. However, it's not hard to find in some organizations managers whose careers seem to go from strength to strength based seemingly on a recipe of aggressiveness and 'seat of the pants' last minute decision making.

So what practical considerations does this raise? Some organizations use a competence framework as a tool for behavioural change. However, if those who consistently display negative behaviours in the workplace are seen to be rewarded by the organization, this can easily lead to a degree of cynicism about the assessment centre process: 'It doesn't count: they've already made up their minds'.

Other related criticisms of competencies are that they are not proactive or forward-looking: they do not reflect the skills and abilities organizations may need for the future. Rapidly changing organizations, it is suggested, should concentrate more on assessing the learning skills of employees. It is only in more stable environments, runs the argument, where it is appropriate to assess existing skill sets.

Competence frameworks are not necessarily 'one size fits all'

Most frameworks are broadly based on an Anglo (Western European/North American) culture. However, with the increasing globalization of business there has been growing interest among both academics and practitioners in the differences in organizational behaviour in different countries and across different cultures. This is potentially a huge topic but one simple example should serve to make the point. Countries with a high 'power distance' characterized by large differences in the distribution of power where it is less appropriate for staff to challenge the 'boss', can often have different views of 'Interpersonal Skill' and 'Leadership' than those presented in the sample framework. Conflict may be dealt with much more indirectly through intermediaries to 'save face' than suggested by the more direct approach of the behaviour indicators in 'Interpersonal Skill'. Similarly, there may be an expectation of a more directive style of leadership than the more situationally-based, flexible style indicated in the 'Leadership' competence. You may need to revise or adapt the competence framework you use to more accurately reflect the cultural norms of the country or region you are operating in.

So which framework is best?

You will find that, whatever the source of your competence framework, each has a number of advantages and disadvantages. When selecting a competence framework for your assessment centres you have three broad options.

Option 1. Your own organization's framework

If your organization already uses a competence framework for performance management and appraisal, seriously consider tailoring the behaviour indicators for use in assessment or development centres. These revised indicators need to retain the essence of the particular competence but reflect the behaviours that will typically occur in the various activities. This will take some time initially, but more than pays dividends in the improved reliability of the assessment process, particularly if you carry out assessments regularly.

Option 2. A publicly available framework

Easily available but, as with option 1, usually written to cover a number of purposes, not just assessment centres. As with option 1, this may well require some tailoring.

Option 3. The sample framework

This framework has been designed specifically to capture the typical behaviours likely to be displayed in the various activities in this book. Often behaviour indicators written for a more general competence framework are used for a variety of purposes, including performance appraisal as well as selection. These can be difficult to assess in a simulated work sample activity or exercise. For example, a behaviour indicator such as 'monitors trends using past data' under the competence of 'Analytical Thinking' may well be reasonable to look for in the context of a 12-month period in a specific job setting, but less realistic during the shorter time span of the simulated activities in assessment centres.

Therefore the sample framework is, consciously, limited in its use. It is designed to assess mainly universal, with some occupational, competencies at the *supervisory/first-line management level* in the very specific context of a series of work sample activities. However, in simple terms, it is 'fit for purpose'.

Many occupationals and relationals have not been included. Neither have competencies that may be more easily assessed using other methods. For example, 'Attention to Detail' and 'Numerical Ability' are more effectively assessed through ability tests (see Chapter 5) and may not apply to all supervisory roles. Similarly, from the excellent MSC framework, skills such as Thinking Strategically, Networking, Information Management, Compliance with Legal Regulatory Ethical and Social Responsibilities and Managing Budgets, have not been included in the sample framework. Some may not apply to the target group level whilst others apply to more specialized roles.

Table 2.1   Sample framework

Positive/Effective	Negative/Less Effective
1. Oral Communication	
Speaks clearly	Mumbles
Speaks at an appropriate pace	Speaks quickly
Keeps to the point	Verbose
Uses straightforward language	Uses jargon inappropriately
2. Written Communication	
Style and tone are appropriate for the situation	Inappropriate tone
Arguments/decisions are presented clearly	Key points or decisions are not clear
Logical structure and flow	Uses no, or inappropriate, structure
3. Presentations	
Uses visual aids as appropriate	Uses visual aids as a 'script'
	Over-uses visual aids
Keeps eye contact with the whole audience	Looks away or only at the audience selectively
Projects voice	Cannot be heard clearly by sections of the audience
Invites audience participation	One-way communication
Uses appropriate structure with an introduction and summary	Has no introduction or summary
4. Customer Service	
Asks questions to identify customer needs	Offers solutions without exploring the issues
Generates rapport/empathy by use of appropriate body language and voice tone	Unsympathetic; avoids eye contact
Balances customer needs with personal or organizational objectives/goals	Allows customer needs to take precedence over personal or organizational objectives
Considers the needs of a range of potential customers (internal and external)	Suggestions do not consider impact on others
Makes realistic proposals to customers	Makes unrealistic promises
5. Adaptability	
Resilient when faced with setbacks; continues to contribute appropriately	Withdraws when faced with setbacks or resistance
Changes approach as appropriate	Keeps inappropriately to one approach/tactic

Positive/Effective	Negative/Less Effective
6. Initiative	
Takes a lead in making suggestions	Relies on others to initiate actions
7. Analytical Thinking	
Spots inferences in arguments	Makes inappropriate assumptions
Distinguishes information relevant to the task	Introduces information not relevant to the task
Keeps the overall objective in mind	Focuses on less critical details
Considers both the benefits and risks of a particular course of action	Acts on suggestions without analysing (dis)advantages
Makes links to spot trends in diverse information	Considers information in isolation
8. Creativity	
Challenges constraints by looking for different interpretations	Accepts constraints at face value
Suggests novel or unusual solutions and approaches	Suggestions are based on the 'tried and tested'
9. Interpersonal Skill	
1. Assertive when faced with difficulty or differences:	1. Aggressive when faced with differences:
a. Non-verbally, eg leans forward, keeps eye contact	a. Cuts others out of the process, eg sarcastic
b. Verbally, eg calm level tone, states clearly what he or she wants or thinks	b. Blocks others' proposals
2. Listens actively:	2. Passive when faced with differences
a. Asks others to contribute	a. Non-verbally, eg avoids eye contact
b. Summarizes others' contributions	b. Verbally, eg sounds hesitant
c. Builds on the suggestions of others	c. Suggestions get 'lost'
10. Influencing	
Backs up suggestions and opinions with relevant data or evidence	Suggestions are inappropriately based only on personal opinion
Compromises as appropriate	Digs in to own position ('yes, but')
Uses emotional appeal as appropriate	Voice tone projects indifference or lack of enthusiasm
Talks about 'common ground'	Talks about differences

Table 2.1   continued

Positive/Effective	Negative/Less Effective
11. Planning and Organizing	
Takes time to review when faced with difficulties	Presses on with an initial plan regardless of difficulties
Suggests an informal plan	Moves to the task with no attempt to plan
Monitors time regularly	Does not mention time
Accurately completes tasks to time	Fails to complete tasks to time and standard
Distinguishes between important and urgent tasks	Defines urgent tasks as important
12. Performance Feedback	
Involves the other person by asking challenging questions (coaching)	Presents feedback predominantly through one-way communication; only asks 'What do you think?' at the end of feedback
Feedback is objective and supported by behaviours	Feedback is subjective or vague
Feedback is owned	Refers inappropriately to others ('I have been told')
13. Leadership	
Involves others as appropriate, eg by asking for ideas and information	Takes over unnecessarily, eg imposes own ideas
Allocates tasks appropriately by setting standards/guidelines for allocated tasks and follows up	Allocates tasks with no follow-up
Acts decisively when appropriate and backs up with reasons (eg time pressure)	Hesitant; directions are unclear or not made at the appropriate time
Keeps the overview (eg overall objective, time)	Excessively 'hands on', eg gets involved in unnecessary detail
Allows others to work out solutions as appropriate	Takes decisions without reference to or confirmation from others

Table 2.2   Which exercises assess each competence?

Competence	Suggested Exercises
1. Oral Communication This competence contrasts to Interpersonal Skill in that it looks to assess the participant's clarity of communication in a broad range of situations. Interpersonal Skill is more specific and looks to assess the style of dealing with differences or conflict	In essence this competence could be assessed in any of the activities in Chapters 8, 11, 12, 13 or 14. Be cautious about over-assessing this competence. The traditional interview is also a very effective method for measuring this competence
2. Written Communication	Role play 1 (Chapter 8). All activities in Chapters 9 and 10. The report-writing activities in Chapter 10 will provide the most comprehensive evidence for this competence
3. Presentations	'Transport Manager' (activity 3 in Chapter 10). Presentations could also be added as an additional task to the other activities in Chapter 10
4. Customer Service The focus in the activities is mainly on the internal rather than external customer. The idea of the internal customer is that managers should regard other departments and staff, either those affected by their decisions or who they offer a service to, as customers	Role plays 1 and 6 (Chapter 8) In tray 3 (Chapter 9) 'Transport Manager' (activity 3 in Chapter 10)
5. Adaptability	Role play 6 (Chapter 8). This competence is most effectively assessed when the shifting constraints concept is used in the activities from Chapters 12, 13 and 14. In many of these exercises it is also worth looking for the reaction of the participants if an original plan is clearly proving not to be working, say in the construction phase of activities such as 'Construction Tender' or 'Bridge Building', (activities 1 and 2 in Chapter 12) or if an incorrect answer is given to the assessors in exercises such as 'Who got the Job?' (activity 5 in Chapter 13,) or 'Flight Roster' (activity 4 in Chapter 14)

Table 2.2　continued

Competence	Suggested Exercises
6. Initiative	This competence is best assessed in the group activities in Chapters 11, 12, 13 and 14 when there is no allocated leader
7. Analytical Thinking	Role plays 1, 4 and 6 (Chapter 8). 'Delegation' (activity 2 in Chapter 11). This competence is most effectively assessed using the activities in Chapter 10. It can also be assessed in some of the group activities, say for example 'Cash Register' (activity 2 in Chapter 13). However, be cautious about relying on group activities to assess this competence Each participant needs an equal opportunity to display the skill. A participant who is, say, weaker in 'Interpersonal Skill' and as a result does not display 'Analytical Thinking' skills should not be doubly penalized
8. Creative Thinking	Role play 5 (Chapter 8). Chapter 9 activities (in trays). 'Charity Allocation' (activity 3 in Chapter 11). All Chapter 12 activities. 'Letter Cards' and 'Broadcast Appeal' (activities 1 and 4 in Chapter 13). 'Committee on Anti-social Behaviour' (activity 1 in Chapter 14). As with 'Analytical Thinking' be cautious about relying on group activities to assess this competence. Each participant needs an equal opportunity to display the skill. A participant who is weaker in 'Interpersonal Skill' should not also be penalized for failing to display 'Creativity'
9. Interpersonal Skill	Although not always specified, any activity that has the potential to generate differences of opinion can be used to assess 'Interpersonal Skill'. This includes all the activities in Chapters 8, 11, 12, 13 and 14
10. Influencing	The role plays are the most effective vehicle for assessing 'Influence' as each

Competence	Suggested Exercises
	participant has an equal opportunity to display appropriate skills: Role plays 2, 3, 5 and 6 in Chapter 8. Also activity 3 in Chapter 10, 'Transport Manager' (Presentation phase). Influence can also be assessed in the group activities, particularly those in Chapter 11, which rely on more open, subjective arguments. Look also at 'Programme Planning' and 'Broadcast Appeal' (activities 3 and 4 in Chapter 13) and 'Committee on Anti-social Behaviour' (activity 1 in Chapter 14)
11. Planning and Organizing	The in tray activities in Chapter 9 provide the best evidence of the behaviour indicators 'distinguishing urgent and important tasks'. Some of the other behaviour indicators can really only be assessed verbally, so have been included as suggested competencies in several group activities: all activities in Chapter 12, activities 1, 3 and 4 in Chapter 13, and activities 2, 3 and 4 in Chapter 14. However, as with 'Analytical Thinking' and 'Creativity', be cautious about relying on group activities to assess this competence. Each participant needs an equal opportunity to display the skill. A participant who is weaker in 'Interpersonal Skill' should not also be penalized for failing to display 'Planning and Organizing'
12. Performance Feedback	Role plays 1, 3 and 7 in Chapter 8. Chapter 6 includes a stand-alone activity designed to assess 'Performance Feedback'
13. Leadership	This competence can really only be assessed through the group activities in Chapters 12, 13 and 14 when one participant is allocated the role of group leader at the start of the activity. If the activity is 'leaderless', 'Initiative' becomes more appropriate

Key tips

- If possible *do not* use a generic competence framework in assessment centres. Adapt or devise a competence framework for use in assessment centres which contains only behaviour indicators likely to be displayed in the activities whilst retaining the essence of the generic competencies. The extra time this takes will be repaid through increased effectiveness of assessment.

- Behaviour indicators need to be brief, clear unambiguous, and relate to observable behaviours.

- Make sure your competence framework fits 'culturally'.

- Assess a *maximum of three* competencies per activity.

- Assess each competence at least twice.

3

Designing and Running an Assessment Centre

Choosing the appropriate competencies to assess is the first building block in designing a successful assessment or development centre. A variety of ways to help you do this systematically and effectively were set out in Chapter 2. This chapter will, therefore, concentrate on other key issues in designing and running assessment centres, including:

- the time required;
- how to most effectively use the activities in the book;
- what needs to be communicated to participants at the various stages of the process;
- how to evaluate the effectiveness of the process.

What is the optimum time needed for assessment?

For many busy HR professionals the practical question when designing an assessment process is, 'How much time do I need to devote to the assessment process?' To an extent this is a 'How long is a piece of string?' question. Let's look at two options.

On the one hand it is entirely feasible and appropriate to simply add one or two relevant activities to the more traditional interview process. Obviously, from an administrative point of view, this is easier if these are individual exercises such as the activities in Chapters 9 (In Tray) and 10 (Analytical/Report Writing). Candidates simply need to attend at an earlier time and be briefed on the individual activities. The only extra resource needed then is a quiet, private room for candidates to work in. For group activities, all the candidates would have to attend at the same time which would, for some, mean having longer waiting times for interviews later in the day. However, it may be possible to use some of this 'dead time' for some individual exercises.

At the other end of the scale a well structured and organized assessment lasting no more than *one day maximum* will be able to provide you with a wide range of extremely valuable information in addition to that gained in an interview setting. Assessment centres can take almost any length of time, but at some point there will be a diminishing return on resources.

If you decide to use one or more of the role plays from Chapter 8 then a potential administrative problem is how to keep the other candidates productively occupied whilst the role plays are being conducted. Although it is unlikely that any candidate would openly complain about having too much spare time you will want to present an image of a professional, well organized process, particularly to any external candidates. Keeping candidates occupied throughout the day not only provides you with the maximum possible evidence on which to base your assessment but, in a fairly realistic manner, reproduces the pressure of many busy workplaces. In these circumstances consider briefing candidates on all activities at the same time at the start of the process. They are then given one overall block of time to complete a number of tasks. An example is given in Table 3.1. This assumes five participants and uses role play 1 from Chapter 8 in addition to in tray 3 in Chapter 9 and 'Crew Scheduling' activity 1 in Chapter 10.

Table 3.1 Making optimum use of time. Sample timetable

Timings	Activity
9.30 – 9.50	Introductions and the organization of the process
	Sample wording: Throughout the day you will be asked to complete a number of activities designed to give us information about your skills and abilities. These are:
	▨ a meeting where you will discuss a problem with a staff member; ▨ two written follow-up responses to this meeting; ▨ an analytical report; ▨ an in tray.
	Full instructions for each activity are given in the briefing sheets on your table. Some suggested timings are given for each of these activities but, with the exception of the role play meeting which will be kept strictly to a maximum of 20 minutes, you will be expected to manage your own time and have all activities completed by 12.10. Please feel free to also take any necessary breaks and refreshments within this time.
	You will each be given a specific time to attend the staff member meeting in room 1.
	Candidate 1 Role Play : 10.10 Candidate 2 Role Play : 10.30 Candidate 3 Role Play : 10.50 Candidate 4 Role Play : 11.10 Candidate 5 Role Play : 11.30
12.10	All written work to be completed

This approach does have the disadvantage that candidates can extend the amount of time they take to complete a task. In this example candidates are now given an extra 10 minutes to complete the tasks when compared to the combined individual timings. Not a particularly large difference, except that candidates are now free to choose their own allocation of time across the activities. They could spend, for example, more than 30 minutes allocation on the in tray if they find this particularly challenging.

What to consider when using the activities

General guidelines

At the end of each activity you will find some information that will help you to run the activity easily and effectively. This includes the following.

1. Suggested competencies to be assessed

These are suggestions only; you may want to substitute other competencies. The idea of competence is that job performance is seen in terms of behaviour rather than the outcomes of behaviour. One potential problem that this throws up for assessment centres is the '*exercise effect*'. This occurs when assessors rate participants in terms of the outcomes of an activity rather than the particular behaviours displayed. This can result in participants receiving different ratings for the same competency when assessed in different activities. Intuitively we would expect that if someone is, say, a skilled and competent communicator that they would display this behaviour across different activities. It seems, however, that the actual outcome of the activity can unfairly influence the ratings of behaviour. Taking the activities in this book if, for example, a group scores a high number of points in one of the group exercises then, according to the exercise effect, this may lead assessors to improve the various competence ratings irrespective of the actual behaviours displayed.

So how can we reduce or eliminate the exercise effect? There is considerable evidence that it can be reduced by having fewer dimensions assessed in each activity. Do *not assess more than three* competencies in any one activity. Also, try to make sure that each competence is assessed at least twice over the course of your entire selection process. Of course, one of the tools you use may be an interview and/or a psychometric test (see Chapter 5). Also, *specify as clearly as possible the dimensions to be assessed*. In reality this means writing clear and precise behaviour indicators, as outlined in Chapter 2, and training assessors in their application.

2. Materials required

One of the criteria used in choosing the activities has been their ease of use. Activities that require expensive or specialized equipment have not been considered, and in general most activities simply require the various briefing sheets, paper and pens. This section is, therefore, only included when activities require more than these basic materials.

Many of us are now much more used to producing written communication using a computer. For activities that require reports of more than a few lines of writing, for example those in Chapter 10, you may want to consider giving candidates access to computers. In order to ensure absolute fairness candidates should *not* be allowed to use their own laptops, unless they are giving a pre-prepared presentation. This may require you to source several laptops.

3. Managing the exercise

Again, this section is only included if there are any special points to be aware of in the activity. In general, however, for all exercises *keep strictly to the allocated timings* and collect written work in accordance with the instructions. For example, do not allow extensions if groups have not completed tasks due to an oversight, if it is 'Planning and Organizing' that is being assessed. To ensure reliability, be as consistent as possible.

4. Assessment/debrief

Debriefs will probably be most appropriate for development centres and are discussed in detail below.

Running specific activities

Group activities

Group size

For the group activities (Chapters 11 to 14), a group size of between three and five is the most effective, although this is not a rigid constraint. Activities such as Charity Allocation and Redundancy (Chapter 11) can be run with more than five participants. However, having more than five group members can limit the opportunities for participants to get actively involved, while less than three means fewer chances for a group dynamic to emerge. The activities in Chapters 12 and 13 are designed to be run for two or more teams working in an informal competition. They can, however, easily be run for one group, but some of the points, such as those awarded for 'quickest' and other forms of competition, may need to be amended or removed.

Group composition

In general, it is more appropriate to keep teams intact throughout the group activities. Whilst it can be interesting in terms of 'Interpersonal Skill' or 'Adaptability' to see how new members fit into a group, it can equally be useful to keep groups together as this is more likely to result in barriers coming down and, if real conflicts emerge, it will be possible to see how they are managed over several activities.

Exercise constraints

The activities in Chapters 12, 13 and 14 contain a number of rules or constraints, with associated penalties if they are broken. It needs to be clearly established that these should take the status of safety rules in the workplace. In other words, it is *not an option to deliberately break these rules and pay the penalty.* If a group is continually breaking some rules then an assessor will need to make a judgement call about when and if to intervene to stop them.

Shifting constraints

The group activities in Chapters 12, 13 and 14 contain an optional element termed 'shifting constraints'. These are alterations to some of the basic instructions contained in the activities. They are designed to throw a 'spanner in the works' and see how the group reacts to last-minute changes. To ensure reliability in the process, shifting constraints need to be used in either all or none of the group activities you choose for a particular assessment centre. Shifting constraints are particularly useful if 'Leadership' or 'Adaptability' are being assessed.

Leaderless or nominated leader?

If 'Leadership' is one of the competencies you are looking to assess then it is critical that each participant has an opportunity to be formally designated as a leader for at least one group activity. Assuming you have six participants you would then need to run three group activities with two groups of three participants.

If you have an odd number of participants, one participant should be asked to lead the group in two activities. The assessors could decide who to nominate if, for example, there is a candidate they have contradictory or mixed evidence about and on whom they would like to gain additional evidence. Alternatively, if one candidate suffered from extreme 'nerves' when leading the group it may be appropriate to give this person another opportunity to lead the group. Remember, however, that this may give this individual an unfair advantage as other candidates would be assessed on their first, and only, attempt. So, whilst this may be good in terms of empathy and PR it may not be so appropriate in terms of reliability.

If no candidate clearly emerges as an obvious person to take on the leadership role twice, it can be interesting to let the group decide amongst themselves. Some highly pertinent interpersonal skills may emerge as the group works to a decision!

Role plays

A key issue that needs consideration is the briefing of role players to ensure a consistent approach. Some organizations use professional actors for this role. Their training allows them to quickly get underneath the 'skin' of a particular brief, ad lib appropriately and yet be consistent. Specialized agencies can provide actors but, of course, there is a cost involved, so many organizations use internal resources. The CIPD website contains a useful section on 'Using theatre in training', which also provides a list of UK companies that provide actors who can be used in various organizational initiatives. The Introduction to this book contains a list of HR representative bodies in other countries that will be able to recommend similar non-UK organizations. However, for non-professional role players, it is critical that they are consistent in all meetings and with all participants. To help with this, provide detailed briefing sheets such as those contained in the role play activities.

Role play 6 (Chapter 8) differs from the others in that it allows both roles to be taken by candidates. The obvious benefit of this approach is that it saves on resources, allowing two candidates to be assessed in the time it would normally take to assess one. However, if one candidate 'dries up' this does not allow the other candidate a reasonable opportunity to display her or his skill. In these circumstances it is acceptable to allow participants a brief 'time out' to reconsider their approach, although the assessors should not offer any assistance or pointers whatsoever.

Is it appropriate to assess outside the formal activities?

At times you may well be able to gain valuable additional evidence about participants outside the confines of the formal activities. For example:

- When asking a team to nominate a group leader.

- From the reaction of members at the end of a group activity, particularly if the exercise has not gone well. Do they push the blame on to someone or something else or honestly reflect on their performance?

- From the reactions of one team if they have successfully completed an exercise well within the time allowed but another team is still struggling to complete the exercise. Remember the aim of the group activities is to score the maximum number of points, not necessarily to 'do down' the other team.

- From how the team reacts if new members are introduced to the group.

Does the order of the activities matter?

Evidence from assessment centre research suggests that the ordering of the activities, with the possible exception that some candidates seem to perform less well in afternoon activities, does *not* make a significant difference to performance. You can, therefore, choose to start with a role play, group activity or report-writing activity. The key design criteria then should only be the efficient use of resources throughout the event.

Communicating with participants

Before the event

In addition to the usual administrative arrangements (location, timings, purpose, arrangements for feedback, prior preparation, etc) it is probably good practice to confirm that it is not seen as appropriate to discuss the details of the centre beforehand and that the assessor team has been instructed not to talk about the process. Whilst this may not stop participants seeking tips and advice from any source they see as useful, it ensures that the 'keepers' of the process themselves are neutral, 'above board' and working to ensure reliability. For development centres, on the other hand, it is *vital* that participants are fully briefed by their line managers. There is considerable evidence that this improves 'buy-in' to the whole process.

At the start of the event

A thorough introduction should include the following aspects:

- Introduction of the assessor team and each participant. Keep this brief and to the point; life histories are not required. For the assessors, name and role. For participants, name, role and section or organization, if appropriate. Some external candidates may wish to keep this confidential.

- The structure of the day and timetable.

- General guidelines for the day. These can be read out or produced as a handout and given to the participants. Try the formats shown below in the two sample introductions.

- Shifting constraints. If you decide to use these as part of the group exercises do not give the detail but say broadly what they are and that they will occur at some point in each exercise.

- Competencies being assessed (optional); see 'During the event', below.

- Arrangements for the notification of results for an assessment centre, or for a debrief and report discussion for a development centre. For development centres it is important to stress that the overall ratings given in a report are *not* a start point for negotiation. There is a natural tendency for participants to focus on the 'score' rather than the evidence, and debate the ratings.

- For an assessment centre, how participants can receive feedback. Giving brief feedback to all candidates is recommended as good PR for both internal and external candidates. The time and effort are more than repaid by the goodwill this can create towards the organization.

Sample introduction 1

'Throughout today you will be asked to take part in a range of activities designed to measure your abilities across a number of skills critical to (name of the role being assessed for). These may be group or individual activities. You will be allowed to ask questions only to clarify information but *not* about how to approach the task. You will be allowed a set amount of time to plan your approach and carry out the task. How you divide your time will be left to you. Once a task has started do not ask the assessors for any further guidance as they have been instructed not to respond to questions or give any further guidance or information. During some activities you will see the assessors writing notes; this does not necessarily mean anything negative or positive. Please try to ignore the assessors and behave as you would normally do in a real work situation. In the group activities there will often be two groups working on the same task simultaneously in friendly competition. Your assessment has *no* connection to your success in the "competition"; this is a fun element only.'

If you are assessing 'Leadership' the following modified format could be used as an introduction to group activities.

Sample introduction 2

'You will be asked, at least once, to lead a team of at least two others in completing a group task. Each activity will follow the same format. You will be given *five minutes* to read a task instruction sheet and prepare your team briefing. You will be allowed to ask questions only to clarify information but *not* about how to approach the task. In each group activity the overall *aim is for your team to score the maximum number of points possible.* You will be allowed a set amount of time to brief your team, plan your approach and carry out the task. How you divide your time will be left to you. Once a task has started do not ask the assessors for any further guidance as they have been instructed not to respond to questions or give any further guidance or information. You will see the assessors writing notes; this does not necessarily mean anything negative or positive. Please try to ignore the assessors and behave as you would normally do in a real work situation. There will usually be two groups working on the same task simultaneously in friendly competition. Your assessment has *no* connection to your success in the "competition"; this is a fun element only.'

During the event

Brief participants about each activity.

Group activities

If 'Leadership' is one of the competencies being assessed brief the leaders together exercise by exercise. Take the participants designated as the group leaders for that particular exercise to one side, preferably outside the main room if possible, but at least out of earshot of the rest of the participants, and give them the task briefing sheet. Make sure only *one* briefing sheet is available per leader. Part of the skill of the leader is to be able to communicate relevant and appropriate information to the team. Allow the leaders a maximum of five minutes to read the briefing sheet. Only answer questions relating to language, not process. Try to remain as 'neutral' as possible. Respond with, 'That's up to you' or, 'You will see that when you start the exercise', if you feel participants are asking for inappropriate guidance. If appropriate this can also be recorded under a competence such as 'Interpersonal Skill'. Whilst one assessor is briefing the leaders it is helpful if another is distributing any materials needed in the exercise.

If 'Leadership' is not being assessed, give each participant a briefing sheet. Allow up to five minutes for participants to read it. Try *not* to answer questions. It can be helpful to say, 'All the information you need is in the briefing sheet'. Only clarify any phrases that non-native English speakers may not understand. Do *not* discuss the possible approaches participants may take. Alternatively, you may choose to read the instructions aloud either with participants following from their individual sheets or with no briefing sheets. Not providing briefing sheets is unusual and rarely has any benefit unless you need to assess memory or note-taking ability! This method might be used to assess 'Creativity' or 'Adaptability', but much more appropriate activities are available. Again it is crucial that, whatever the briefing method chosen, it is applied consistently.

Other activities

Timings and detailed instructions are included in all the briefing sheets.

Other information

For development centres, give a list of the competencies being assessed along with behaviour indicators at the start of the day. Before each activity, recap briefly the competencies to be assessed. For assessment centres, on the other hand, do *not* specify either the competencies or behaviour indicators being assessed.

Intervening during the activities

This is, in general, to be avoided, and does not encourage objectivity in the assessment process. However, as discussed earlier, at times you may need to remind groups of some constraints if they are continually being broken.

Debriefing

Debriefing is generally only appropriate if an activity is being used as part of a development centre. After each of the activities the most usual questions to ask are:

- What went well for you?
- What were you less comfortable/happy about?
- What would you do differently if you were asked to do this task again?

The participants' openness, honesty and skill in self-reflection will dictate the amount of challenge and direct feedback the assessors will need to give. In the face of negative or less successful outcomes, participants will often use 'situational attributions' (see Chapter 4) by looking to external causes as the reasons for failure: 'I'm not like this at work', 'The exercise was not realistic', 'The instructions were confusing', or even be overly positive about their team's performance. The 'assessment/debrief' section for each activity outlines the key points that generally emerge from the exercise.

During development centres it may also be appropriate to utilize video recording for the role plays. If using home video standard equipment it is often difficult to distinguish the specific contributions of each individual in group activities. Allow participants to view any recordings in private rather than playing them back in front of a large group as this reduces anxiety and possible embarrassment.

In general it is inappropriate to debrief activities when used as part of assessment centres. On occasion, however, you may find it useful to ask participants questions at the end of activities. It may be that you would like a group to provide a rationale for a decision they have made in order to assess 'Analytical Thinking', for example Cash Register (Chapter 13). You may, alternatively, want to get more information about 'Influencing' by questioning group members about why they had changed their minds on a particular issue. This technique is particularly appropriate for open-ended activities where an individual phase is followed by a group phase. Examples are Redundancy and Delegation (Chapter 11), and Committee on Anti-social Behaviour (Chapter 14). The key issues to consider are: 1) will this give consistent evidence against the competencies being assessed in this activity, and 2) how can we ensure consistency across assessors?

Evaluating the process

BPS best practice guidelines on assessment centres recommend monitoring the outcomes arising from assessment/development centres. The review of the process should take place periodically and include adequacy of content coverage, equality/diversity issues, and data gathering with statistical evaluation.

Although getting the time to actually do this may well be tricky, evaluation can pay for itself in terms of reflecting on the effectiveness of the

process. It can also act as a check that equal opportunities legal requirements are being met. At a bare minimum you need to set up a straightforward system to be able to capture data such as competence scores and
candidate demographics from assessment and development centres.

Sample evaluation report

This report refers to data collected from a middle management development centre. Able and Watson Glaser (see Chapter 5) are both ability tests.
'Situational Leader' is a leadership style questionnaire. It is based on a
contingency model that suggests that the most effective leadership style,
ranging from highly directive to delegating, is based on the situation the
leader finds him or herself in.

Able scores are close to those of the test publisher norm groups, in contrast to
a similar comparison for Watson Glaser Critical Thinking Ability scores. This
suggests that Able is an appropriate test for this group.

Able scores differ significantly in terms of department and nationality. Those
from the sub-continent and Service departments scored significantly higher
than those from other groups. However, given some of the small sample sizes
the results need to be treated with caution.

There are a number of statistically significant differences in the overall
ratings for the six competencies. This suggests that, as assessors we are marking
to the competence definition rather than the outcome of the exercise ('exercise
effect') or other personal bias.

'Planning and Organizing' and 'Analytical Thinking' scores are identical,
suggesting there may be some issues of construct validity here. Are we assessing
the same core construct and do we need clearer definitions of the differences
between the two?

The preferred leadership style in terms of both self and boss perceptions is
coaching (style two). There is, statistically, no correlation between self and boss
perceptions of leadership style. This is not in itself an issue or problem. Overall,
however, there is a shared perception between bosses and the development

centre participants as to preferred leadership style, with bosses' scores being more 'evenly' spread across the four styles.

Situational Leadership scores have some variance in terms of sex, males assessing themselves as significantly more directive (style one) than females and less likely to use a supporting style (style three).

Key tips

■ A maximum of one day is, generally, sufficient time to thoroughly assess a range of competencies. Plan carefully so that candidates are fully occupied during the assessment.

■ Assessors should, on the whole, not intervene during activities.

■ Organizational skills are key to ensuring consistency. Without a consistent approach to briefing and debriefing, reliability can easily become compromised. Make sure that:

- role players are trained;

- you have a lead assessor to make sure the day runs smoothly;

- you have an informal script for assessors to use.

4

Assessor Skills

As we discussed in Chapter 1, a potential issue in the delivery of effective assessment centres is how to ensure reliability and consistent assessment by different assessors and at different events. This chapter looks at some of the key skills of assessing and gives some tips to ensure assessors are consistent in their ratings of participants.

What makes a good assessor?

To be able to run assessment centres on a regular basis you will need to select and train a small team of assessors.

Assessing requires the skills of:

- remaining 'neutral';
- listening and concentrating;
- group decision making.

In development centre processes, assessors also need to be able to give feedback and write reports.

Remaining neutral – biases in assessment

Often our biases are unconscious: we may not even be aware of them. However, they can have a powerful effect on our decisions. Biases can either be individual, termed *cognitive* or *social*, in that they emerge in group decision making.

Cognitive biases

The effects of non-verbal information on judgement

Examples include dress, height, physical features and perceived attractiveness. There is evidence from research studies that candidates who are taller, or are even seen as more attractive, are more successful in job applications. Some of the processes that underlie these effects include:

- *Categorization/stereotypes.* These are mental short-cuts that help us to simplify, classify and make sense of the world, and there is often sufficient truth in them for them to be useful within certain bounds. Stereotypes operate when a single characteristic of an object or person suggests to us a group of other qualities supposedly linked to that characteristic. For example, married people are more responsible and stable, or younger people learn more quickly. Stereotypes can cause us to prejudge in the absence of evidence, and can operate like self-fulfilling prophecies in that they lead us to act towards people in a way that brings out the trait we expect them to have. Prejudice is an extreme example of the operation of stereotypes, where a negative evaluation is made of a person solely on the basis of a single characteristic such as race or sex. Whereas few people can honestly claim to be free of all prejudices, it is important that assessors heighten their self-awareness of possible prejudicial attitudes in order to minimize the unjust impact on individuals – and to avoid potential legal consequences.

- *Temporal extension.* This occurs when a fleeting expression is judged to be an enduring feature of behaviour. For example, someone who smiles once or twice is judged to be always happy.

- *Parataxis.* This involves generalizing characteristics from someone we know to someone who reminds us, physically, of that person. For example, a participant may physically remind us of a friend known for her sense of humour. We then infer the same sense of humour to the candidate.

- *Functional quality.* This occurs when linking the functions of parts of the face to aspects of personality. For example, someone with big eyes can see into others' motivations.

Information overload

When assessing, this occurs because the information processing task is complex. As the number of competencies increases, accuracy decreases. This can lead to the 'exercise effect', discussed in Chapter 3, where correlations of ratings of the same dimension in different exercises are low. This effect can be reduced by having precisely defined dimensions and also by limiting the number of competencies to be assessed at any one time.

Heuristics

These are simplifying processes that imperfectly mirror reality. One example is *availability*, where unusual or infrequent behaviours are more easily recalled. Another is *anchoring and adjustment,* where we start at an initial anchor or value and then adjust from this point. For example, an assessor may come to a selection process thinking that a particular candidate is strong in certain competencies based on his or her CV data. Any subsequent evaluation starts from this anchor rather than a more neutral position.

Lack of concentration

This occurs because it is very difficult to observe or listen continuously, and human attention is notoriously selective. When concentration lapses, we tend to reconstruct what we think we heard, or wanted to hear. If we have expectations or preconceptions, for example based on hearsay, we may filter out information that contradicts the preconception and only attend to that which confirms it.

The 'halo' effect

This occurs when judgement across a range of different dimensions is contaminated by a single dominant positive quality or impression. The person is therefore judged to be good on all dimensions. The opposite effect, where a single poor characteristic results in an overall negative judgement, is sometimes called the 'horns' effect.

Primacy and recency

This refers to the truism that first impressions stick, often regardless of later evidence. Judgements and decisions about people's characteristics are often made in minutes. Later information that contradicts the initial impression is frequently ignored.

Leniency and central tendency

Some individuals seem to be naturally softer 'markers'. They may not want to generate conflict by giving negative feedback or may like the person they are assessing on a social level and not want to risk offending them. Similarly, some individuals have a tendency to go for the middle ground when rating anything; this is one reason why some rating scales do not provide a 'mid-point'.

Social biases

These are the biases that emerge when assessors are discussing and agreeing their overall ratings of candidates in the final 'wash-up' session. Social influence processes include *conformity pressures*, the pressure to go along with the majority; *status*, deferring to more senior members of the team; *exchange tactics,* 'you agree with me on A and I'll support you on Y'; and *extremity shifts*, a form of group polarization that gives more extreme ratings. Of course, knowing about these biases doesn't necessarily mean you can easily avoid them! As a first step it can be helpful if assessors develop the skills shown in Table 4.2 on page 74. It is also vital that assessors are open and honest in sharing feedback about the group process, either in a wash-up session at the end of the assessment day or in periodic reviews.

Should assessors interact with participants during the activities?

Although it may sound a little obvious to say, it is of critical importance that observers remain completely neutral throughout each activity. This means not responding to any questions or queries once an activity is underway. As outlined in Chapter 3, it is also important to be extremely cautious before an activity starts in answering questions about the briefing sheets, particularly if the participant seems to be asking for guidance about how to approach a task. In the introduction to an assessment or development centre it should be made clear to participants that the assessors will not answer any questions once an activity has started.

If you are asked a question by a participant, possible responses could be:

'All the information you need is in the briefing sheet.'
'That's up to you to decide.'
A quiet smile!

On rare occasions it may be appropriate to intervene. For example, as suggested in Chapter 3, there may be times when a group is systematically breaking a key rule in one of the group activities. Similarly, role play 6 in Chapter 8 involves two participants conducting a meeting. If one participant 'dries up' it is appropriate to give him or her a short time to 're-group' in order that both participants get a reasonable opportunity to display effective behaviours.

If you are using one of the group activities from Chapters 12 or 13 there may be occasions when one group has successfully completed a task whilst another group or groups are still working. In these circumstances remain neutral and state that 'the full exercise is completed after X minutes'. The assigned observers should continue to monitor the group to look for their reaction. Do they critically reflect on their performance or is there a mood of superiority and 'one-upmanship'. Although it is rare to get systematic, behavioural evidence, some interesting behaviours can emerge, particularly when participants feel they are no longer 'under the microscope'.

What's the best way to record observations?

Observations must be based on behaviour. The assessor's task is to observe:

- what each participant did non-verbally;
- what each participant said, or omitted to say;
- details of time including periods of silence.

Focusing on actual behaviour has a number of benefits:

- Themes of style and approach can emerge. A person's oral communication may be effective when he or she is relaxed but deteriorate noticeably when under pressure. A more detailed picture emerges, therefore, when behaviour from different exercises, observed by different assessors, is compared.

- It provides specific examples to justify ratings. Each participant in a development centre should be provided with a written report as well as overall ratings. Whether to give feedback after an assessment centre is very much down to the choice of the individual organization. Providing feedback, either verbally or in writing, is often positive PR for the organization, particularly if external candidates are being assessed. However, there are some obvious resource implications in providing feedback. If the final report and feedback to the participant are based on actual behaviour this usually increases the participant's acceptance of the feedback.

- It gives the basis for *objective discussion* between assessors. Opinions and interpretations are subjective and it can be hard to debate them meaningfully. It is easier to reach a consensus about the significance of behaviour than about an impression.

Possible recording errors include:

- making general statements: 'He was directive' or 'She was well organized';

- assuming you know *why* somebody did something: 'He asked for ideas because he wasn't sure what to do';

- assuming you know what someone is feeling: 'He was frustrated with Ms A';

- describing personality characteristics: 'He is an extrovert'.

The assessor's observations will eventually be used to make ratings against competencies and as evidence in feedback. Therefore, observations must be accurately recorded. Recording will usually take place while actually observing, so it will not always be possible to record every detail of observed behaviour, especially in group activities where the assessor may be observing two or more participants. The assessor will have to record key words and actions.

Ways to record observations

Recording of participants' behaviours is one of the key aspects of the assessor role. Two methods have been outlined for you to consider.

First, you can record directly on to an observation form, as in the example shown in Table 4.1.

When designing these forms, try to use as small a font as possible for the behaviour indicators as this will give the maximum possible space in the middle area for observers to record comments. Tailor a separate sheet for each activity and keep to a maximum of two sides of A4 for all competencies assessed in the activity. Any more would result in assessors drowning in paper!

Table 4.1 Observation construction form assessing 'Planning and Organizing' in activity 12.1, Construction Tender

Takes time to review when faced with difficulties	*'Let's review our objective'* (after shifting constraints were introduced)	Presses on with an initial plan regardless of difficulties
Suggests an informal plan	*'Could we take a few minutes to read the sheet without any discussion with the team?'* *Picks up paper and starts to build before sharing ideas*	Moves to the task with no attempt to plan
Monitors time regularly	*On one occasion only. 'There's eight minutes before the construction phase'*	Does not mention time

The advantage of this method is that it avoids the time-consuming process of going back and coding evidence later. It also allows judgements to be made close to the event. The key disadvantage is that it can slow down the recording process. The assessor needs to observe a behaviour and then, before recording it, decide what competence and which behaviour indicator it relates to. This requires a lot of mental processing and in the time it takes to do this other information may be 'lost' or overlooked. It may also unconsciously encourage or lead the assessor to come to an overall judgement before the assessment process has been completed. If this happens, evidence gained later in the process could be coded to justify a decision that has already, subconsciously, been made.

The second, commonly used method is to simply write down, verbatim, what was actually said in as much detail as possible. In contrast to the first method this obviously allows more evidence to be recorded. However, it means that the assessor will need to revisit his or her notes and code the evidence in terms of competence and behaviour indicator. This takes additional time and relies on the assessor remembering the context in which any particular remark was made and any appropriate responses.

Coding individual evidence

As already discussed in Chapter 2, even the most specific competence framework will still require assessors to demonstrate a considerable degree of judgement in deciding where and how to code specific behaviours. A principle to follow is to look at context and reactions.

Context

In a group activity a behaviour such as asking for another participant's opinion may be positive at the start of an activity ('involves others as appropriate' in the 'Leadership' competence) but could easily become a less effective behaviour at the end of the exercise if the group was struggling to meet a time deadline ('avoids acting'). The phrase 'as appropriate' in many behaviour indicators suggests assessors need to take the context into account when coding behaviours.

Reactions

How do other people react to a comment or statement? If we are going to evaluate a comment such as 'sarcastic', did the person it was aimed at become quiet as a result, respond with a similar remark, or just 'laugh it off'?

Making an overall rating

In discussing final overall ratings, often referred to as the 'wash-up' session, three key factors need to be taken into account:

1. *Frequency.* The number of times and consistency with which a particular behaviour was displayed.

2. *Strength.* A participant may only use, for example, an aggressive behaviour once throughout an assessment. However, if the reaction and effect (see above) are critical, for example if another participant who had been highly involved withdraws completely, then this would be much more significant in terms of an overall rating than a greater number of more minor examples of the same behaviour.

3. *Avoid penalizing or crediting twice.* This potential error has already been discussed in relation to specific competencies in Chapter 2. However, it bears repeating, particularly in relation to group exercises. A participant weak in 'Interpersonal Skill' or 'Oral Communication' can be unfairly penalized if, as a result, he or she is then unable to display appropriate behaviours in another competence such as 'Planning and Organizing' or 'Analytical Thinking'. Make sure each participant has an individual opportunity to display these behaviours in addition to those provided in the group activities. Otherwise use a rating of 'no evidence given' rather than a negative rating.

To ensure consistency it is also important that the assessors have as clear an idea as possible of what constitutes a particular rating. General definitions are acceptable in the context of a report, but assessors need clearer guidelines to inform their final discussion. In the following guide for 'Interpersonal Skill' (competence 9 from the competence framework included in Chapter 2) the following overall ratings were used:

4 = Outstanding.
3 = Competent.
2 = Development needed.
1 = Minimal application/no evidence provided.

Interpersonal skill sample scoring guideline

A 4 score describes a participant who consistently displays a range of interpersonal behaviours, particularly active listening.

A 3 score should be given for a participant who may display interpersonal skills such as assertiveness in many situations but display aggression selectively, for example in the role play or when under pressure in a group activity.

A 2 score is used when there is concern about consistent use (in other words across two or more activities) of poor interpersonal skills such as aggressive or passive behaviours. Additionally, the participant could be consistently defensive during debriefs ('not like work', 'yes but...').

A 1 score is reserved for any participant who rarely, if at all, displays interpersonal behaviour. For example, he or she may be quiet throughout the majority of the activities and not contribute, even when invited to by other participants.

Obviously this guide still involves a degree of interpretation. Other guides can be more 'objective' depending on the activities used. The following example relates to 'Analytical Thinking' (competence 7) in an assessment that also included an ability test.

Analytical thinking sample scoring guideline

For a 4 score the candidate needs to obtain a raw score of at least 50 in the ability test. In addition, the candidate would focus on one or two critical issues in the role play and keep the big picture in mind in the group activity.

A candidate who gains a raw score of 44–50 (average score) would probably generate an overall score of 3 assuming there was no consistently negative evidence in the other exercises.

A raw score of 43 or lower would really have to generate a 2 score. Strong evidence of using information appropriately in other exercises may mean that a candidate who scores 40–43 could be given an overall 3 rating. Candidates who score lower than 40 should be given a 1 score.

The ability test is the *strongest evidence* for this competence.

It is strongly recommended that you devise your own overall rating scale or system. Although this can take some time it is an essential aid to ensuring reliability in your assessments. This should provide: 1) a guide for collating evidence from several sources under one competence. This might include guidance such as whether one activity should be seen as providing a stronger rating or if all activities should be considered as being equally weighted; 2) pointers for making an overall rating. Keep your system simple. A three-point scale with a fourth category for 'no evidence' should be sufficient in most cases.

How should disagreements and differences be resolved?

Unfortunately there is no magic formula for this. Assessors need to be skilled in competencies such as 'Influencing', 'Interpersonal Skill' and 'Analytical Thinking'. However, as a rough guide, *avoid the social biases* identified earlier and *keep the 'big picture' in mind* by starting the discussion of each candidate with a broad overview. Ask questions such as, 'Do we have any concerns about participant X?' rather than going immediately into detail and discussing specific behaviours for each competence. This can slow things down considerably. If differences emerge then it is at this point that it is more appropriate to move the discussion on to specific behaviours.

Table 4.2 Assessor behaviours in group decision making

Effective	Less Effective
Drawing conclusions from several pieces of connected data	Drawing conclusions from one piece of evidence
Linking data to relevant competencies	Applying personal views of effectiveness
Interpreting candidates' behaviour from more than one cultural perspective	Interpreting candidates' behaviour from his or her own cultural perspective
Discussing candidates in terms of evidence observed during assessment	Introducing hearsay and opinions from non-assessment sources
Involving colleagues by asking for information	Imposing opinions
Listening to others, for example by asking questions to clarify	Digging in when faced with alternative views

Giving feedback

Effective feedback, whether delivered verbally or in writing, needs to be objective and specific and avoid judgmental language. This means, as outlined earlier, using as many behavioural examples as possible. Feedback should also be balanced, including both strengths and areas for development, and provided as soon after the assessment event as possible. When delivering feedback verbally keep a neutral expression.

Written feedback/reports

Detailed written reports are most usually associated with development rather than assessment centres. Participants should always be given the opportunity to discuss a report to clarify any areas of uncertainty and also to start thinking about any development planning. It is important that the discussion does not become a negotiation about ratings. At the start of any development centre it should be made clear to the participants that the overall ratings are not a matter for negotiation and that it is essentially the specific comments that are the most valuable part of the report. A sample feedback form is given in Table 4.3.

The end product of any development centre should be a detailed development plan with clearly identifiable goals. These can include a range of activities such as:

- Classroom-based training programmes provided either by in-house training or external companies. These can range from short skills-based courses to longer qualification-based programmes such as an MBA.
- Online learning.
- Self-study such as distance learning for a qualification or reading relevant books.
- Guided reflection, which is a particularly useful option to consider for areas where it is difficult to anticipate and plan development activi-

Table 4.3 Sample feedback report

Competence	Rating	Observations
Interpersonal Skill	2	Peter displayed a range of behaviours in this competence.
		In the X group exercise he was extremely task-focused, preferring to experiment with various practical designs, and therefore appeared somewhat passive or uninvolved in the group discussions.
		In the Y group activity Peter may have been more effective by challenging the choices of the other group members. He tended to 'go with the flow' in order to make an easy and quick decision, even though time was available to continue the discussion. In contrast, during the role play meeting he was assertive on a number of occasions, for example in pinning down the line manager to some deadlines, emphasizing the importance of safety and in summarizing the discussion. When giving peer feedback he was also assertive in that he addressed a number of development issues calmly and confidently.

ties, for example assertiveness and conflict management aspects of interpersonal ability. Typically this will involve taking two or three relevant situations such as handling an angry staff member and assessing how effectively you think each was handled. *Written* notes need to be made for the follow-up discussion. This activity works particularly well in combination with classroom based learning and online learning.

- Delegated tasks or assignments, as in Table 4.4.

- Observation and feedback. This might be of a presentation or of the staff member conducting an interim review and could be conducted by a coach or mentor.

- Shadowing. If you think this would be a useful tool you need to specify who, why and what the written output will be from this activity.

Table 4.4 Developmental assignments

Activity	Example
Small projects and start-ups	Proposal report to senior management
	Supervise purchase of large item
	Plan an off-site meeting
Fix-its	Design new, simpler procedures
	Manage group of inexperienced people
	Supervise cost-cutting
Small strategic assignments	Write a proposal for a new system
	Write a policy statement
	Study innovation of competitors
Coursework or coaching	Train as an assessor
	Teach a workshop
Activities outside work	Become active in a professional body

Which is the most effective method?

Several research studies have suggested that projects or assignments that stretch the individual, in association with appropriate coaching, were regularly seen by managers as the most effective in their development. International research by Development Dimensions International, covering 15 countries worldwide and published in its Leadership Forecast 2003, listed the following activities in terms of their perceived effectiveness. Special projects or assignments were seen as the most effective, followed by in-house formal workshops, discussing/analysing skills with another person, external formal workshops, tests/assessments or other rating of skills, articles/books, computer-based learning, and participating in community or non-work activity.

Follow-up

For any of the activities outlined above to be effective there needs to be at least one follow-up meeting. This could be with a line manager, who would therefore be acting as a *coach* in this situation. Alternatively a *mentor,* typically someone not from the same department, could be used. Depending on the actual activity a number of possible questions could be discussed:

- What has the staff member learnt about him or herself (strengths and weaknesses) through this activity?
- What has she or he learnt in terms of knowledge or skills?
- What further support would be helpful to continue this development?

Any activities in the development plan *must* include a date for a follow-up/debrief meeting.

'SMART' objectives

When discussing methods of improvement try to keep them:

*S*pecific
*M*easurable
*A*chievable but still stretching
*R*ealistic
*T*ime-bound

When constructing SMART objectives keep in mind that the end point of a developmental objective is not necessarily 'now developed... no problems', but could be the completion of a defined range of tasks.

Sample developmental objective

Complete 'Employee Performance Providing Feedback' online learning within three weeks. Note three key skills of coaching and discuss briefly with manager within two further weeks.

Within the next two months conduct two interim performance reviews with line manager sitting in as observer. Within a further week obtain verbal feedback from manager on questioning style.

SMART objectives have a number of advantages:

- there is greater chance they will be acted on as there are specific targets;
- if targets are realistic, they are more likely to be met, giving a sense of achievement and further motivation;
- they give the manager something concrete to follow up on, if appropriate.

Verbally

You may find that you encounter some resistance to developmental issues during verbal feedback. This can, in part, be explained by *attribution theory*. Attributions, or locus of causality, are the reasons we give for actions. Attributions can be broken down into three aspects:

1. Internal (dispositional)/external (situational). Internal attributions are based on characteristics of the person, and may include attitude, personality or skill. External attributions centre on the situation, for example vague instructions, unfair assessment or pressure. There is a powerful tendency in negative situations for actors, the participants at an assessment, to explain their behaviour in terms of the situation yet for observers, here the assessors, to use dispositional explanations.

2. Stable/unstable. A stable cause is one that will probably continue over time ('I'm an aggressive person') whilst an unstable one is likely to change ('I was in a bad mood at the assessment centre'). Participants are much more likely to use unstable attributions ('I had a really bad cold') to explain poor performance.

3. Global/specific. Global explanations tend to cover other areas of life ('I panic under pressure') as compared to specific attributions ('I'm not good at timed tests'). Again, participants are more likely to explain poor performance through specific attributions ('I'm not good at acting in these role plays').

These differences can be explained by three factors:

1. *Perspective.* The differences in attribution can be because of differences in what we see. The observer is looking at the actor. Usually it is the actor's behaviour that gains more attention than the situation, which is relatively static. The actor, on the other hand, is not looking at him or herself, but at the situation. In all interactions we are looking at each other from different perspectives. We are likely to have a different understanding of what is going on partly because we are looking at different things.

2. *Information.* The observer usually only has information from a limited number of events. He or she, therefore, has to generalize from that. The actor has information about his or her own behaviour over longer periods of time. For instance, the actor knows that on some occasions he or she behaves in an assertive way and at other times not.

3. *Motivation.* One of the main reasons we need to attribute is to be able to control and predict our environment. Explaining a person's behaviour in terms of their personality enables us to anticipate their future behaviour, and to organize our own behaviour accordingly. Actors, on the other hand, want to maintain their freedom to behave in different ways to meet the demands of each new situation, and so prefer to see their behaviour as a flexible response to the situation, rather than the function of the same behaviour pattern. There is also evidence that those who use dispositional attributions to regularly explain negative events can be more prone to mental illnesses as they are more likely to be overly self-critical and blame themselves excessively when things go wrong. So situational attributions for negative events can, in fact, be not only normal but also healthy!

Why is attribution theory useful?

Attributions help us to understand why it is not unusual to encounter resistance to negative feedback. Of course, knowing this does not make the resistance disappear. However, it can help in viewing the participant's responses as, in many ways, natural rather than being tempted to describe her or him as being difficult or 'negative'. Other ways to minimize or tackle resistance are:

- Use as many specific behavioural examples as possible in your feedback.

- Involve the participant in the feedback by using a *coaching* style of feedback. Evidence suggests that participants see decisions as 'fair' if they are involved in them in some way. This is referred to as 'procedural justice'. Coaching involves asking a number of open and challenging questions rather like the debrief questions described in Chapter 3: Where do you think you did well/poorly? What would you say the effect of that was? What examples do you have of that?

- At some point, however, for example if the participant becomes increasingly defensive or disputes each point, it is also appropriate to present feedback calmly, assertively and in a direct manner without inviting comment from the participant. At development centres do *not* get involved in a negotiation about individual ratings.

Where can I get assessors from?

In practice this often boils down to anyone who volunteers, or can be persuaded to volunteer. One volunteer is worth a thousand forced staff! In organizations the selection of assessors is often determined by many factors in addition to skill and suitability. Assessors are most usually chosen from the HR/recruitment teams. For development centres in particular, staff from the functional department are also used in the process. This encourages 'buy-in' and commitment from the 'user' department, ensures increased face validity of activities if these staff are also encouraged to get involved in the design phase and, in general, adds to the perception that the process is not just another HR initiative.

The arguments you can use to persuade colleagues to join the assessor team are obviously fairly individual. You might try approaches such as:

- It will be good for your personal development; this could be one more string to your bow.
- The skills are generic and can be easily transferred to, and enhance, some core supervisory and managerial functions such as performance feedback and appraisal.
- There are proven statistical improvements in selection gained by using assessment centres.
- It's interesting in itself.
- Bargaining: if you get involved I can help you with...!

What training do assessors need?

Training of assessors, both specialists and those from user departments, is vital. Research evidence has shown that this clearly improves inter-rater reliability, ie consistency in ratings amongst different assessors. This should ideally take the format of a briefing about a specific process or event. Generic assessor skills training, whilst helpful, is not as effective as training tailored to a particular event. However, either type of training needs to have a strong emphasis on skills practice. *One full day* should be sufficient to fully brief participants on the role of an assessor and give them an opportunity to practise the skills of assessing. Of course the more practice and feedback the better, but one day should provide a good start point, and is probably a realistic time to expect busy line managers to be absent from the workplace. An outline programme for a one-day assessor workshop should therefore include training in behavioural observation, rater errors and rater biases. It is essential to include as much practice as possible in your assessor briefings. You can use either videoed activities or ask half the participants to assess the other half carrying out activities, then swap the roles.

Divide assessors into pairs or small groups and let them assess 'mock' participants completing a range of the activities to be used in the actual process. Have each group make independent 'blind' ratings without discussion then compare the decisions. In the debrief discuss issues such as leniency, central tendency and skewed ratings (halo/horns).

You can also prepare participants by asking them to assess a character in a short, less than 10 minutes, extract from a DVD. If you have access to training videos these can be a good source. Alternatively, choose something from a TV drama. You might also consider a 'home-produced' video of a training activity, for example one of the activities included in this book; role plays work best. The key criterion in choosing the extract is to make it 'neutral', not so obviously good or bad that assessing is too easy or obvious. You need something that will, hopefully, stimulate debate. Once you have chosen the clip you need to script the words and actions of your character and provide a 'model answer' in terms of coding each piece of evidence. This can take some time to prepare – a five-minute clip can include up to 40 different pieces of evidence – but pays huge dividends in terms of assessor effectiveness. Participants will then assess the chosen character using the actual competencies and behaviour indicators from the process the training is aimed at. The debrief can touch on issues of recording evidence and biases in assessment, using the information presented earlier in this chapter.

It can also be effective as part of this training to analyse real notes made at assessment centres in terms of their effectiveness. For example, ask the group to look at comments such as:

'X was a good leader and controlled the group well.'
'Y asked A for her opinion on three separate occasions.'
'A was overly aggressive.'
'D reminded the group of rule number two.'

Participants should then rate the comments in terms of their effectiveness as assessor notes. In other words, are they specific and based on behaviour rather than being judgmental or too general?

How can I best deploy assessors during the assessment centre?

In the group exercises it is vital that candidates are observed by specific assessors throughout the span of the assessment and that assessors rotate between participants. To make sure this happens easily and systematically, draw up a simple grid outlining which assessors will be observing which participant(s) in each activity.

Having a 'free for all' where assessors watch all candidates simultaneously means that, in group activities, attention is inevitably drawn to the more talkative participants. Often valuable evidence can be gained by consistently observing quieter candidates. Do their facial expression and body language suggest they are involved and engaged with the process or have they perhaps withdrawn for whatever reason? Rotating participants between assessors also avoids the risk of a decision being made solely on the judgement of one person.

There is no set ratio of assessors to participants. Obviously the greater the number of participants an assessor is expected to observe the less evidence that can be recorded accurately. As a rough rule of thumb, the effectiveness of any process that requires an assessor to observe more than two participants at any one time is likely to be compromised. It is strongly recommended that you appoint a 'lead assessor' who is responsible for the organization of the event, briefing of candidates and generally overseeing the smooth flow of the event.

The example shown in Table 4.5 assumes a panel of four assessors with eight participants. Four group activities are used so that each participant is given the opportunity to formally lead a group.

Table 4.5 Sample assessor observation grid

	Activity 1	Activity 2	Activity 3	Activity 4
	5.1 Construction tender	*6.1 Letter cards*	*5.3 River crossing*	*6.5 Who got the job?*
Assessor A	Blue Group Participant 1 (nominated leader)	Blue 3	Red 1	Red 3
Assessor A	Blue 2	Blue 4	Red 2	Red 4 (leader)
Assessor B	Blue 3	Blue 1	Red 3 (leader)	Red 1
Assessor B	Blue 4	Blue 2 (leader)	Red 4	Red 2
Assessor C	Red Group Participant 1 (nominated leader)	Red 3	Blue 1	Blue 3
Assessor C	Red 2	Red 4	Blue 2	Blue 4 (leader)
Assessor D	Red 3	Red 1	Blue 3 (leader)	Blue 1
Assessor D	Red 4	Red 2 (leader)	Blue 4	Blue 2

Assessor A: (Lead Assessor): Rani
Assessor B: Sanjeev
Assessor C: Amy
Assessor D: Noel

Key tips

- It is essential to train assessors.
- Assessors should, in general, not intervene during activities. An exception may be if some of the rules in a group activity are being systematically broken.
- When recording evidence, consider factors such as strength, reaction, context and frequency.
- Make sure participants with weaker 'Interpersonal' or 'Communication Skills' are not then also penalized for failure to display other skills such as 'Analytical Thinking' or 'Planning and Organizing'.
- Devise your own rating scale. Keep this simple, with no more than four categories.
- When giving feedback try to coach, but also know when to move to a more directive style.

5

The Role of Psychometric Instruments in Assessment and Development

You may well have taken a psychometric test at some point in your career. A significant majority of respondents to the 2006 CIPD Recruitment, Retention and Turnover Survey indicated that they used them 'to some degree'. This usage is replicated internationally and tests are also increasingly being translated into languages other than English. However, there is a wide range of opinions about the usefulness of psychometrics. These range from those who believe they are an essential part of any assessment to those who feel they are 'psychobabble' on a par with newspaper horoscopes in terms of their accuracy and usefulness.

The purpose here is to give a broad overview of some of the issues associated with using psychometrics in assessment and development centres. This will leave you in a position to make more informed decisions about how, when and if you feel psychometrics can add significant value to your processes.

What are psychometrics?

The BPS defines a psychometric test as 'an instrument designed to produce a quantitative assessment of some psychological attribute or attributes'. OK, but what does this boil down to in more everyday language? Psychology is a science that attempts to explain how people behave and think. In common with other sciences, psychology develops theories about concepts such as ability and personality. Any 'metric' is a measure of something, so psychometrics are measures of attributes or qualities such as ability and personality. What all of the instruments share in common is that they are a standardized set of questions that have been designed to measure some very specific aptitude, ability or personality characteristics.

Instruments should always be administered in a standardized test setting, in other words the process should be the same each time. Results are then interpreted in terms of where the test score places the taker in comparison to an appropriate group of people who have taken the test before. It is this standardization and use of comparison to large groups of people that allow more accurate inferences to be drawn about the individual's aptitudes, abilities, attainments or personality characteristics.

Psychometric instruments can, broadly, be divided into three groups. Within each group there are many different tools, as discussed below.

1. Aptitude and ability tests

These tests are designed to measure general mental ability and some specific occupational abilities. General mental ability includes:

- verbal reasoning; higher-level verbal reasoning tests might measure aspects such as drawing inferences, recognizing assumptions and evaluating arguments;
- numerical reasoning;
- non-verbal or abstract reasoning, using diagrams rather than figures or words;
- mechanical and spatial skills.

Occupational abilities include, for example, checking, filing, spelling, problem solving and aptitude for computer programming, amongst others.

A recent development that might be included under ability testing, as they involve 'correct' responses, is the use of Situational Judgement Tests (SJTs). Here candidates are presented with work situations and asked to choose from various responses in much the same way as they might answer, verbally, a hypothetical question at an interview.

Sample SJT question

You have become aware that a co-worker has been stealing considerable amounts of office supplies. A colleague told you that this person has already received a warning about this once before. You have just seen several boxes of printer cartridges in the back of her car in the company car park. Mark which responses you feel would be the most and least effective:

- Politely tell your co-worker that you will inform the manager the next time you catch her taking office resources.
- Report the incident to the manager.
- (Up to five options.)

---

2. Personality inventories

There is a large variety of personality instruments that reflect differing models or beliefs about human personality and behaviour. The California Psychological Personality Inventory (CPI), Fundamental Interpersonal Relations Orientation–Behaviour (FIRO–B), Myers-Briggs Type Indicator (MBTI), 16 Personality Factors Version 5 (16PF5) and Occupational Personality Questionnaire (OPQ) are some of the more well known and internationally used instruments and each has its supporters and detractors. However, there is a growing consensus that the structure of personality is represented most satisfactorily by the 'Big 5' personality dimensions and it is usually possible to 'fit' constructs from popular instruments into one of the Big 5:

1. *Extroversion* relates to social orientation – the degree to which we want to be around people, to be noticed and put energy into starting and maintaining relationships.

2. *Stability,* which is also sometimes called *anxiety* or *neuroticism,* although this latter phrase has some unfortunate implications for mental health! This refers to the degree of problems an individual has in coping with everyday situations. Those higher in stability are more likely to be calm, composed and satisfied with their lives.

3. *Openness,* sometimes called *tough mindedness,* is a thinking style. Those low in openness are more likely to be realistic and practical. Their decisions are less likely to be affected by feeling and emotions. They prefer the tried and tested. Those high in openness, on the other hand, prefer to work with ideas and have the opportunity to devise new or creative approaches to problems.

4. *Independence,* which is also known as *agreeableness.* This refers to the extent to which individuals are influenced by others and the force with which they express an opinion. It also describes the desire to get things done or make things happen. Those high in independence are less concerned with cooperation and social harmony.

5. *Conscientiousness* or *self-control* describes how an individual responds to environmental constraints. Those with high conscientiousness are bound by, and conform to, group standards of behaviour. They are more likely to control and regulate their impulses.

The Big 5 are sometimes referred to by the mnemonic *OCEAN:*

*O*penness
*C*onscientiousness
*E*xtroversion
*A*greeableness
*N*euroticism

3. Interest inventories

These inventories are designed to help people understand their professional or occupational preferences. Instruments within this category are primarily used within career guidance and counselling contexts and it is unusual to find them used in selection. Some psychologists see occupational preferences as a function of personality, suggesting that there are really only two types of psychometric test, and indeed many personality inventories include a 'derived' scale of occupational preferences.

However, there are also a number of motivational questionnaires that measure the need for rewards, status, achievement, positive relationships, independence or responsibility. Although we might be interested in the motives of applicants, there are two problems associated with using these types of instruments in selection. They are relatively easy to 'fake' and, as stressed in Chapter 1, we are primarily interested in observable behaviour during assessment, not necessarily what causes it.

Should psychometrics be included as part of an assessment process?

Ability tests

In Chapter 1 criterion validity was identified as one of the key factors in choosing a particular selection method. Criterion validity asks whether the inferences we make from a selection method are justified. Usually this is some aspect of job performance, although other criteria could be used, such as training performance. Ability tests generally have good validity and, if matched to the appropriate competence, are good predictors of performance. So what type of ability test might be appropriate for the types of skill and competencies in the sample framework introduced in Chapter 2?

This book provides tools to assess competence at the supervisory/first-line manager level. The most appropriate ability tests to consider using are verbal, numerical or abstract reasoning tests. They should be aimed at the graduate or professional/managerial level and can provide valuable evidence to assess the competency 'Analytical Thinking' (competence 7). Most test publishers offer verbal, numerical and abstract reasoning tests. Specific examples are the Watson Glaser Critical Thinking Appraisal and Psytech's Reasoning Abilities Test series. Sample reports for these tests are given at the end of the chapter. Other competencies not included in the sample framework such as 'Attention to Detail' can also be effectively assessed using appropriate ability tests.

A note of caution should be struck here. The fit between a test and a particular competence is, at best, an intuitive guess. Often there is not a 100 per cent fit between the skill assessed in a test and the competence as defined. The only way to be sure that a test is a good predictor of job performance is to carry out a criterion validity study. However, in organizational settings these are time-consuming and costly, so it is common for some educated guesses to be made!

Personality inventories

Whilst evidence is mixed, personality inventories generally show poor criterion validity. When results from studies are combined, in what is known as a 'meta-analysis', only self-control/conscientiousness seems to be associated with aspects of job performance. Of course, we need to be cautious about generalizing too much. These figures may well alter, depending on job type and the job criterion being predicted. However, it is relatively rare for there to be a statistically significant correlation between high performers in a particular job and a particular personality profile.

On reflection these results are not terribly surprising. Personality inventories are designed to measure personality rather than job performance. You may remember that in Chapter 1 we talked about construct and content validity. Personality instruments have very good content and construct validity. If a researched personality instrument claims to measure, say, extroversion, you can be fairly sure it does. However, a statement such as, 'When I go to parties I speak to as many people as I can', may well tell us about a person's level of extroversion but whether it makes that person more interpersonally skilled, for example, is open to debate. As we saw in Chapter 1, there are many influences on behaviour in addition to personality. We would not expect a thermometer, excellent though it is at measuring temperature, to accurately measure pulse rates! Personality profiles are based on self-ratings which, in addition, raises the fundamental question of the degree to which each of us can be really said to be aware of our personality.

Unfortunately there is a temptation in many organizations, particularly by those not properly trained in occupational psychology, to make unfounded, intuitive, 'common sense' connections: 'This job involves meeting the public, therefore I need people who score high on warmth'.

You may feel that there is a double standard operating here. Why is it fine to use ability tests based on intuitive fit with job performance but not personality profiles? The key point, however, is that the evidence that does exist, such as that from meta-analyses presented in Table 1.1 in Chapter 1, strongly supports the validity of ability tests as predictors of job performance whereas it is much weaker for personality tests.

So, in this light, do personality profiles have any role to play in selection and development? Yes, as long as they are used properly, ethically and with appropriate caution. In selection, this can be to highlight areas of concern, possibly to be probed in an interview, or as secondary sources of information to support other methods with stronger criterion validity such as ability tests and work samples. It might also be that if the available work samples do not give evidence for the competencies being assessed, a personality inventory may prove to be invaluable. An example might be if we want to get an idea of how an individual copes with change, which is hard to design a work sample activity for. Finally, the evidence suggests that conscientiousness is linked to work performance and is, therefore, worth measuring as a predictor of effectiveness. Personality instruments can also be extremely useful in the 'lower stakes' context of a development centre where they can provide powerful insights to behaviour patterns.

In the end 'you pays your money and you makes your choice'! The only sure way to know if a personality instrument adds value to your specific selection process is, as for ability tests, to conduct a criterion validity study. In simple terms this involves finding out if the personality profiles of high performers in a particular role are statistically different from those of low performers. This requires input from a qualified occupational psychologist, is both time-consuming and costly and, therefore, not practical for many.

Sample criterion validity report

Two hundred high and low performing staff were scheduled to attend a day of testing; 177 attended. They completed a battery of tests which, in addition to 16PF4, included a personality inventory, Gordon Personality Profile GPP-I, Rotter's Locus of Control, which indicates the extent to which individuals feel events are either within or outside their control, and the Differential Aptitude Test (DAT), which is a test of abstract reasoning. In addition, 16PF4 data when taken at initial recruitment for 83 of the staff was also analysed.

Of the Big 5 global personality factors, Anxiety (emotional adjustment) and Control had statistically significant associations with the job performance in the role.

The most powerful combination is GPP-I Responsibility with 16PF factor O (retest) which, when combined as a discriminant variable predicted around 70 per cent of the high/low classifications.

16PF4 taken at initial recruitment proved to be an extremely poor predictor of performance with no significant associations found between individual factors and performance or by grouped factors (discriminant analysis) and performance.

Reasoning ability has a weak association with performance.

Performance was not predicted from non-personality factors such as age, sex, nationality or tenure/grade, either individually or in combination.

Factors associated with globals, extroversion, openness and agreeableness had no predictive value.

GPP-I generates more associations between scores and overall provides a more robust predictor of performance in comparison to the other three instruments trialled. This may well be because one of the stated objectives behind the design of the GPP-I was to produce an inventory that is resistant to distortion.

Reliability of 16PF is moderate; 9 out of 16 factors showing significant correlation between entry and retest. Interestingly, three of the four factors contributing to the global factor anxiety (C, O, Q4) are stable, suggesting that, for this sample, anxiety may be a product of personality rather than situational factors.

Internal reliability of 16PF (retest) was *extremely poor* with none of the six factors tested (A, C, G, O, Q3 and Q4) having acceptable alphas.

What are some of the issues in using psychometrics?

Reliability. How often is it necessary to test?

This is something of a controversial issue when personality inventories are used as a selection tool. One applicant for an internal promotion in a large hotel chain was amazed when she was asked to retake a battery of personality inventories just over six months after she had taken the same tests. The recruiter told her that because she was now three days over the six-month cut off, the tests were not considered reliable even though the applicant confirmed she still felt her old profile to be accurate. Four days earlier, however, and she would have been OK! Guidelines vary but usually suggest that, for selection, inventories over one year old are not reliable; but pick up the user or technical manual of any well constructed personality inventory and you will find a battery of impressive statistics to confirm its reliability. One frequently used measure of reliability is 'test–retest', which measures the extent to which results change over time. Given that personality is generally accepted as an enduring individual characteristic it should be no surprise that published inventories are reliable.

There is an argument that some aspects of personality are determined by certain situations and therefore should be regularly reassessed. For example, of the Big 5 described above, stability, which includes constructs such as apprehension and tension, may well change according to circumstances. However, recruiters can't have it both ways. If an instrument is considered inaccurate after six months then why would any organization want to use such volatile information to make a selection decision, particularly in light of the several months lead time typical of some recruitment? Cynics might suggest that regular retesting can only be good for the profits of test publishers! Others argue that retesting is partly political in that organizations may be reluctant to accept that individuals are not malleable and cannot be developed to attain the highest levels of performance. Indeed line managers may also at times want to avoid the potential conflict of giving negative feedback and hide behind the impersonal, detached 'objectivity' of the psychology specialist.

However, as with all debates there are two sides to the story. Retesting after a year can be seen as more of an ethical than a statistical issue. Whilst accepting that people tend not to change dramatically, runs this argument, we must accept that change is possible. It is, therefore, ethically important to consider the person as they are now, rather than, say, 12 months ago.

Bad practice and application

Some of the supposed failings of personality instruments are as much to do with the way they are applied as with the instrument itself. In the UK both the BPS and the CIPD have published codes of practice for the use of psychometric tests. The ITC (International Test Commission) has produced international guidelines that follow similar lines. These suggest that personality inventories should not be used for initial screening and that appropriately delivered feedback including written reports should be provided. Good practice emphasizes that personality profiles *must* be presented to the takers as a series of hypotheses: 'You describe yourself as more detached than others. How does this strike you?' This gives the taker the opportunity to provide his or her own view and explore the implications of the profile. On occasions the job interview can be an appropriate opportunity to do this, although this is generally carried out most effectively by a trained test user in a separate session.

A potential pitfall in using personality instruments, although harder to be conscious of, is *pre-judging* the candidate on the basis of a favourable or unfavourable personality inventory. The temptation then is to fit all other information around the description from the inventory. This is an easy mistake for a non-psychologist to make given the 'scientific' trappings associated with the statistics of the test.

Codes of practice suggest that organizations produce a policy statement on the use of psychometric tests. An example is produced below.

Sample policy statement on the use of psychometrics

The term 'psychometric' covers both timed ability tests and personality inventories.

We use a range of psychometric instruments in many of our management development processes. Evidence suggests that these can be a valuable and objective aid to self-reflection and assessment.

Each member of the team is accredited by the British Psychological Society (BPS) to administer and interpret psychometric tests. As such we are committed to working within the BPS guidelines for the fair and ethical administration of psychometric tests.

How do we use the information?

Ability tests, in combination with other assessment tools, may be used to determine an individual's rating in a relevant competence.

Personality instruments are *not* used to generate ratings. They act as the start point for a discussion about the individual's preferred style in a range of management skills. Personality tests are not infallible and the individual may justifiably not agree with an initial interpretation. When used in development centres, other activities may be used to support the initial profile interpretation. Where possible we use computer-generated reports to ensure consistency of interpretation of personality inventories.

Who sees the information?

For ability tests, a brief description of where a particular score places that individual in comparison to others – average, below average, etc – will be included in a summary report sent to the participant and line manager.

For personality instruments, written reports will only be seen by the individual participant. The individual may share the information as he or she feels appropriate.

Psychometric test results are kept *strictly confidential*. They are not kept on any official HR record or shown to other managers.

What happens to the information?

Information is entered into a statistical summary that helps us develop specific comparison groups. No names are entered into this database so the information is kept anonymous.

Individual answer sheets are destroyed after three months.

Inappropriate use of instruments

Only normed instruments, where the test score places the taker in comparison to an appropriate group of people who have taken the test before, are usually used in selection. The norm groups provided by test publishers are usually fairly general, such as 'professional/managerial' or 'males aged 21–30'.

In selection we are, ideally, more interested in comparing test results against those judged to be effective in the same or similar jobs being selected for. However, building in house norms can be time-consuming so usually it is the norm groups provided by the publishers that are used. An example of the inappropriate application of personality inventories is the use, in selection, of preference indicator instruments such as the Myers-

Briggs Type Indicator (MBTI), which do not generate norms. These instruments usually have a forced choice format so the respondent has to express a relative preference between two statements. Indeed the publisher of MBTI, Oxford Psychologists Press, clearly recommends that MBTI should *never* be used in selection.

Is it possible to cheat when taking a personality test?

Faking is obviously not an issue in ability tests that have right and wrong answers. However, personality inventories do not have 'correct' answers. If you were applying for a job working with the public that required 'outgoing individuals able to work under pressure', how might you respond to statements such as: 'I am known as a warm, supportive, caring person' or 'I feel in control of my life'? It is hardly surprising that some test takers attempt to provide what they feel are socially desirable responses, particularly in 'high stakes' situations.

To counter this, many personality tests include some questions such as, 'I have never told a lie, not even for a good cause', which measure *impression management*, an indication of whether a test taker might be trying to present her or himself in a socially desirable light. Standardized briefings that point out the required approach and make clear reference to these 'impression management' scales also help to minimize faking.

Cultural fit

There are two, inter-linked, issues regarding culture. The first practical issue relates to the translation of personality questionnaires into other languages, known as 'adaptation'. In essence the argument is that translating tests is not the same as translating other documents. The language needs to capture the essence of underlying psychological concepts. There can even be issues of translating tests from UK to US English. Think about translating a question referring to an English sport such as cricket. What is the US equivalent, not in sporting terms of a game played with a bat and ball but in terms of what it might mean to test takers? Perhaps something traditional and leisurely? Baseball might not convey the same meaning.

It therefore follows that caution should be exercised in asking those for whom English is a second language, even those who are fluent, to take a personality test in English. It could be that the psychological essence of a phrase does not translate. Appropriately tested mother tongue versions should be used. For example, the 15FQ+, a personality test based on Cattell's 16PF, and for which a sample report is reproduced at the end of the chapter, is available in French, Spanish, Russian, Indonesian, Chinese and Arabic.

The second issue is more fundamental and asks if the Big 5 model of personality adequately describes all aspects of personality in Anglo cultures. For example, some have suggested that the model is not clearly replicated in Chinese culture. Factors that apply only in Chinese culture include concepts such as 'Face', 'Family orientation' and 'Graciousness-Meanness'. Again, like many debates in psychology , there are two side to the coin, with others suggesting that the Big 5 do, in fact, also apply to Chinese culture!

Computer-based psychometric testing

The ITC claims that in recent years substantial and rapid developments have occurred in the provision of stand-alone and internet-delivered computer-based testing. There are three types of use:

1. Uncontrolled and unsupervised, where the test taker registers to take the test on the open internet.

2. Controlled but unsupervised, where the organization making use of the test registers the candidates and ensures their identity, but takes no other action to supervise the timing of the test or the environment in which it is taken.

3. Controlled and supervised, where a qualified test user is required to log in the candidate and ensure that timing and other test require-ments are met.

Computer-based testing carries a number of advantages including controlled administration, accurate timing, reduced supervision, and immediate and accurate scoring with resulting cost and resource savings. Possibly most important is that most test takers seem to prefer online applications.

Leaving aside the possible technical problems, such as power outages, the key question, in particular for online testing, is, 'Are the test results the equivalent of a test administered traditionally?' This is a growing area of research by psychologists and the early indications are that they are. For ability tests, lack of control could obviously lead to issues such as test item security and cheating. However, it seems that software and process solutions such as random choice of questions, one-time-only log on and security questions are being developed to counter these possible drawbacks.

Gaining access to psychometric tests

In the UK access to psychometric instruments is restricted to those with appropriate training. The training required is determined by the BPS through its Certificates in Competence in Occupational Testing, which are divided into Level A and Level B (Intermediate).

Level A is required for you to have access to and be able to purchase ability tests. All test publishers require you to present this certificate when you register with them. However, once you have done this you will be able to purchase and use all of their ability test instruments with no further training.

Level B (Intermediate) is necessary to be able to purchase personality measures. However, the situation is a little more complex than for ability tests. As part of the Level B (intermediate) training most training companies offer access to two personality instruments. These are always instruments for which the company has copyright and distribution rights. If you want to gain access to other instruments but have not undertaken your Level B (intermediate) course with the test publisher, two options may be available. Some companies will accept training in the instrument conducted by other BPS-verified assessors. Others, however, will only grant access to those who complete their own, shorter, 'conversion' courses. It is best to contact the specific test publisher directly to clarify its particular requirements.

The Psychological Testing Centre (PTC; www.psychtesting.org.uk), part of the BPS, provides a directory of training course providers and also a list of qualified test users.

What are the costs?

Training

Prices for a full combined Level A and B (intermediate) training course start at around £1,500 for a programme partly based on distance learning. Costs vary widely for residential programmes, ranging from about £1,300 to over £4,000. Specialized courses such as conversion courses for other instruments generally work out at about £400 to £500 per day per delegate (residential).

Materials

Obviously it is hard to generalize costs across the full range of available tests. However, to get you started using any test you will need to purchase a reference set. This includes a user manual, scoring keys and a number of question booklets and answer sheets. Costs can be as low as £25 for an ability test reference set but are usually in the region of £200 for personality instruments.

Usually the only ongoing costs are for question booklets, in the region of £3 to £4 per copy of the booklet, and answer sheets. These are often produced separately and question booklets are reusable. If you feel that £4 is expensive for what, in essence, amounts to a few pages of A4 paper, please consider the resources needed to conduct the extensive research studies that are required before a test can be ethically marketed as a 'psychometric'.

Many companies offer a bureau service. Scores are sent to the company which then produces a computer-generated report. These cost in the region of £20 to £30 per report depending on the test and report type. Some examples are reproduced below. Computer-generated reports are both quick to produce and, perhaps more critically, reliable, as it is a computer rather than an individual that produces the document. However, to access these services you must be appropriately trained and registered with the test publisher to use the specific instrument. As discussed earlier, personality test results, regardless of the format they are presented in, must always be regarded as interim reports and used as the basis for a discussion with the test taker.

Another flexible option is to purchase the software to allow you to produce computer-generated reports in-house. Software costs in the region of £400 to £800. They generally work through a series of credits that are needed to generate reports. The credits typically work out at about 50 per cent of the cost of the same report generated through a bureau service, making this a cost-effective and flexible approach. The example given below of 15FQ+ would cost £35 using Psytech's bureau service. The Abstract Reasoning test would cost £10.

Testing outside the UK

In the Introduction to this book you will find a list of representative bodies for psychologists in a variety of countries. They will be able to provide the requirements for access to psychometric tests in other countries, lists of accredited training providers, and materials and training costs.

Key tips

■ Test training *is essential* if you plan to use psychometric tests. Even if you initially use external resources to administer and interpret tests, it is strongly recommended that you take these courses. In addition to being the only way to be able to purchase instruments, the training provides valuable insights into the construction and use of tests.

- Ability tests have high criterion validity and are good predictors of job performance. However, carefully consider the 'fit' between the test and the competence being assessed. In addition, the appropriate norm group needs to be chosen. For supervisory and first-line managers, the focus of the activities in this book, this should be a graduate or professional/managerial group.

- Personality instruments are, in general, poor predictors of job performance. They can be very useful as development tools or to help in identifying areas to explore in selection interviews. It is unethical to use personality instruments as a filter in any selection process. Be highly cautious about making common sense assumptions regarding the links between personality and behaviour.

Sample computer-generated psychometric reports

1. Personality Test. 15FQ+

The 15FQ+ assesses the broad personality factors identified by Raymond B Cattell and operationalized in the 16PF. It is published by Psytech International (www.psytech.co.uk).

Form A contains 200 questionnaire items, each with three possible responses: true, false and '?'. For example, 'I am quick to speak up and express my opinions.'

> The 15FQ+ contains a number of measures that examine the way in which the respondent has approached the questionnaire. The response style indicators would suggest that Anne Sample was as happy as most people to present herself openly and candidly, without wishing to project an overly positive image of herself. Please note that response style indicators should be treated with some degree of caution and any suggestions made should always be corroborated during feedback.

Interpersonal style

Anne Sample's personality orientation is quite extroverted. That is, she will like a good deal of contact with people and will adopt quite an open style in her communications. She is likely to feel at ease in the company of strangers, and will tend to come forward in social gatherings. Expressing moderate levels of warmth and empathy, she is likely to be seen as relatively supportive of colleagues. No more or less sympathetic and understanding than most, she will be able to maintain a degree of distance from colleagues when necessary. Her enthusiasm and sense of fun are held in check by a degree of inhibition. In the right setting, she should be as capable as most of letting go and having a good time. Extremely socially confident, Anne Sample will be bold, venturesome and totally uninhibited in social interactions. Seeking high levels of social stimulation and excitement, she is extremely likely to be adventurous and will enjoy being the centre of attention. She will relate easily and comfortably with people and will be drawn to social situations for the recognition it provides, and will have no trouble with 'stage fright' but will not generally rush to be centre-stage. Relatively confident of her intellectual abilities, she is likely to be particularly effusive when discussing lofty issues. Her ability to withstand external pressures without expending too much energy will enable her to face quite gruelling emotional situations. Generally preferring to work within a team, Anne Sample enjoys group participation and social recognition. She will tend to feel most comfortable working in a group setting, where she can share her thoughts with others.

As amenable and cooperative as most, she will generally not seek confrontation for confrontation's sake. Being moderately competitive, she should not be averse to meeting challenges. While capable of being outspoken on occasion, she should not be oblivious to others' sensibilities. Temperamentally, Anne Sample is extremely trusting by nature and sees little reason to be suspicious of others' motives. A high-profile group member, she may occasionally be accused of being too trusting and overindulgent, but is sufficiently forceful not to have the wool pulled over her eyes. Believing strongly that people are genuine and honest, she will usually give them the benefit of the doubt. This strong inclination may make her appear rather credulous and there is a risk that she may be easily taken in. In personal exchanges she is inclined to be very self-assertive, forceful and controlling, with a desire to have her own way. Wilful and potentially aggressive, Anne Sample is very inclined to give vent to noticeably strong opinions and may tend to be domineering. She appears to be as sensitive as most people to the demands of social situations. Her tendency to be direct with people may vary according to her perception of the needs of the situation.

Thinking style

Anne Sample is likely to come across as a somewhat intuitive person who is quite receptive to ideas and experiences. Creatively oriented, she is likely to be somewhat sensitive to the subtleties and nuances of life. She is likely to be viewed as a relatively intellectually-oriented person who enjoys working on complex problems and ideas. Being rather competitive in this regard, she may express her insights in a challenging manner. Having a somewhat conventional perspective on life, she prefers established, well-proven solutions to problems. She may, as a result, be somewhat reticent about accepting new, innovative ideas, particularly if they are outside the realm of her own personal experience. Very soft-hearted and aesthetically sensitive, she is likely to lack a tough, hard-headed, utilitarian approach. Having a very creative and artistic temperament, she will be drawn to expressive activities and cultural elaborations. Very senti-mental and open to feelings, she will be readily moved by emotions of wonder-ment and awe in the face of beauty and sensational events. As attentive as most people to practical realities, she will not be unduly dismissive of abstract, theoretical concepts. She will tend to balance a focus on the here and now with an openness to possibilities and ideas.

Having below average levels of self-control, Anne Sample's behaviour and attitudes are more a function of her own personal belief system than social norms and expectations. Free-thinking and quite spontaneous, she may be somewhat dismissive of authority. Not having particularly high levels of self-discipline or self-control, she is not likely to be overly concerned about her social standing. She may prefer to relate casually to others rather than strictly observe formality and social etiquette. A person's status, position or authority is unlikely to carry much weight with her – she will tend to view people on their merits. However, being diplomatic and aware of the impact she may have on others, these attitudes may not always be evident. Not wishing to spend excessive amounts of time on the detailed aspects of a task, she will be happy attend-ing to detailed systems and procedures if this is a necessary part of the role. As far as rules, regulations and procedures are concerned, whilst she will acknowledge their contribution, she may not wish to be tightly bound by them at all times.

Coping style

Anne Sample is currently experiencing very low levels of anxiety. Relatively emotionally resilient and stable in mood, she should have little difficulty facing challenges in a calm, collected manner. Generally unruffled by events, she is likely to be viewed as being dependable in a crisis. She should have sufficient energy to cope with quite demanding situations. She should generally be able to rapidly recharge her depleted energy resources after having faced demanding work schedules. Relatively secure and considerably self-assured, she is likely to be cheerful, optimistic and free of regrets and self-doubt. Relatively sure of herself and her intellectual abilities, she is likely to appear confident, especially in social settings. If things go wrong she is liable to blame the situation. Anne Sample appears to others to be an easy-going and composed individual. She projects herself as a sedate individual who is not easily perturbed and is not often moved to outbursts of anger or frustration. People may find her relaxed composure in the face of a crisis, reassuringly impressive. Only the most major frustrations and irritations are likely to upset her.

Additional comments

The following section lists a number of points that can be inferred from Anne's assessment report. The interviewer may wish to use these as the basis for further probing during the interview or counselling discussions.

Potential strengths
- Will tend to assert herself and make her views very clear to people.
- Will tend to take into account relevant feelings and emotions when making decisions.
- Will generally appear to be self-assured and confident.
- Will tend to have a high regard for people and is likely to give others the benefit of the doubt.
- Extremely relaxed and self-assured, she may provide reassuring composure and confidence in a crisis.

- Has positive self-regard and highly developed social self-confidence.
- Should be able to quickly respond to a challenge and may enjoy taking risks.

Potential development needs

- May seem somewhat forceful and inattentive to the needs of others in achieving her objectives.
- May experience difficulty in emotionally tough situations.
- At times her self-confidence may be interpreted as complacency.
- May tend to be too trusting and take others at face value.
- May appear to lack a sense of urgency.
- May have a tendency to overlook her own limitations in her approach to situations.
- May be too inclined to take unnecessary risks.

Norms based on a sample of 1186 Professional Managerial staff

Reproduced with permission.

This report also provides information on a number of derived scales such as Belbin's Team Roles. Belbin's research indicated that effective teams contain individuals who can fulfil a number of roles that provide ideas, analysis of ideas, leadership, team cohesion, and the drive to complete projects.

2. Watson Glaser Critical Thinking

The Watson Glaser Critical Thinking Appraisal is designed to measure abilities involved in critical thinking, including the abilities to:

- define problems;
- select important information for the solution to problems;
- recognize stated and unstated assumptions;
- formulate and select relevant and promising hypotheses;
- draw valid conclusions and judge the validity of inferences.

Norm Group: Accountants/Auditors/Bookkeepers/ Financial Analysts

Total score

John Smith obtained a total raw score of 68 out of 80 possible points on the Watson Glaser Critical Thinking Appraisal – Form A.

Percentile score

John Smith's score was better than or equal to 62 per cent of the individuals in the norm group indicated at the top of this report. This individual is likely to excel with the type of critical thinking involved in complex analysis and decision making. Specifically, in comparison with peers from the specified norm group, this individual is likely to:

- Define complex problems and situations clearly and objectively.
- Readily identify subtle and obvious information needed to enhance decision making or problem solving effectiveness.
- Apply sound logic and reasoning when analysing information.
- Consistently draw accurate conclusions from information.
- Develop strong arguments for the support of ideas.

Note. The Watson-Glaser Critical Thinking Appraisal should never be used as the sole basis for making an employment decision.
Reproduced with permission.

Watson Glaser is available in the UK from Harcourt Assessment (www.harcourtassessment.com).

3. Reasoning abilities

The following three aptitude tests assess the candidate's ability to think logically using words, numbers and abstract concepts. They assess the ability to both understand and develop logical arguments and solve complex logical problems. These tests are published by Psytech International (www.psytech.co.uk).

Sam Sample

VR2 Verbal Reasoning

The Verbal Reasoning Test assesses a person's ability to use words in a logical way. Consisting of items that involve an understanding of vocabulary, class membership and the relationships between words, this test measures the ability to perceive and understand concepts and ideas expressed verbally. While this test is a measure of reasoning ability rather than educational achievement, it is nonetheless generally recognized that verbal reasoning test scores are sensitive to educational factors.

Sam Sample's performance on the Verbal Reasoning Test places him within the middle band when compared to the reference group. His score is typical of the comparison group, suggesting that his verbal reasoning ability is as strong as most other people's. While he will be able to understand instructions and explanations without too much difficulty, it may take him a little time to fully appreciate the logic underlying complex arguments. As able as most to use words in a logical, rational way he should be able to explain concepts with which he is familiar with a fair degree of clarity.

NR2 Numerical Reasoning

The Numerical Reasoning Test assesses a person's ability to use numbers in a logical and rational way. The test consists of items that assess the candidate's understanding of such things as number series, numerical transformations and the relationships between numbers, and their ability to perform numerical computations.

Sam Sample's performance on the Numerical Reasoning Test places him just below average when compared to the reference group. This suggests that Sam Sample will find it a little harder than some to understand numerical concepts and that it may take him a little time to fully appreciate complex numerical problems. He should, however, be able to cope with day-to-day numerical work and has sufficient numerical ability to benefit from further training and development.

AR2 Abstract Reasoning

The Abstract Reasoning Test assesses the ability to understand complex concepts and assimilate new information beyond previous experience. The test consists of items that require the recognition of patterns and similarities between shapes and figures. As a measure of reasoning it is independent of attainment and can be used to provide an indication of intellectual potential. Assessing the ability to quickly understand and assimilate new information it is likely to predict how responsive to training the person will be.

Sam Sample's score on the Abstract Reasoning Test shows that he has performed at an average level when compared to the reference group. This indicates a typical level of natural or fluid ability. This should enable him to grasp new and relatively complex concepts outside of his previous experience as quickly as most. With an average capacity to learn he should benefit as much as most from training and instruction.

Norms used

Verbal: 4494 General Population.
Numerical: 4494 General Population.
Abstract: 4494 General Population.
Reproduced with permission.

6

Adapting and Devising Activities

Why devise your own activities?

Surely, you may think, the whole point of purchasing a book of assessment centre activities is to save the whole troublesome business of sitting down and writing your own! However, there are some circumstances where you may want to either revise or create from scratch some exercises:

- You may want to tailor activities to make them more organization-specific to avoid criticisms of lack of relevance, in other words of low face validity. As we saw in Chapter 1, face validity is the appearance, to the person being tested, that the activity is measuring what it claims to measure. However, again as discussed in Chapter 1, it is often much more appropriate to set exercises in a neutral context to avoid criticisms of inaccuracy or favouring some candidates with specialized knowledge.

- Most exercises reach a 'sell-by' date. This is particularly true if a process is used on a regular basis, say when an organization is experiencing rapid growth.

• You may also want to keep the process fresh so that candidates do not come 'over-prepared' although, as we saw in Chapter 1, 'over-prepared' candidates can actually do their chances more harm than good!

This chapter provides:

• practical tips on how to amend and adapt existing activities;

• a guide to devising activities from scratch;

• some additional practical activities;

• discussion on the latest trends in assessment.

Approaches to devising activities

Devising an activity does not, necessarily, mean sitting down with a blank sheet of paper and starting from scratch.

Amending and adapting activities

Minor revisions

You may want to make activities sector/industry specific. Let's take the example of role play 1 from Chapter 8 (participant brief):

> You work for a large hotel chain and are responsible for the front office check-in. You have received a complaint letter from a customer about one of your front-office staff who was allegedly 'rude and aggressive' after a mix-up over a cancelled booking.

This activity could easily be changed by altering the phrases 'large hotel chain' and 'responsible for front office check-in' to another context, as in the first example below, which gives two variations, one for a retail store and a second (in parentheses) for a transport company.

Sector-specific revision, example 1

You work for a large retail store (bus company) and as a floor (call centre) manager are responsible for a number of sales assistants (booking clerks). You have received a complaint letter from a customer about one of your staff who was allegedly 'rude and aggressive' after a mix-up on delivery dates (cancelled bookings).

Alternatively, you may want to assess customer service in the context of the 'internal' customer, particularly if you are recruiting for a job with no direct customer interface.

Sector-specific revision, example 2

You work for a large manufacturing company and as an HR manager are responsible for the company payroll. You have received a complaint letter from the head of another section about one of your staff who was allegedly 'rude and aggressive' after a mix-up on a bonus payment.

In this case, task two (in role play 1) would also need to be reworded to read: '2. a letter you would subsequently write to the line manager of the other department.'

Similarly, you could alter the timing in this exercise from 20 to 15 minutes to introduce more pressure to the situation. If you wanted to use the role play as a training activity, you could increase the time to 25 minutes.

Adding extra tasks

It is often possible to take a basic exercise and add extra tasks thereby extending the number of competencies being assessed. Let's take a practical example from the 'Crew Scheduling' activity in Chapter 10. As presented, this is an individual exercise designed to assess 'Written Communication' and 'Analytical Thinking'. However, the basic activity could profitably be extended to include extra tasks such as a group discussion and a presentation.

In the case of a group discussion, after the individual phase participants would work in small groups, up to a maximum of five, to agree a group solution to the activity. Possible competencies to be assessed might include 'Oral Communication', 'Interpersonal Skill', 'Influencing' and 'Planning and Organizing'.

Sample wording for additional group task

As a group you now have to agree the best solution. You need to provide the assessor with a clear written solution including costs. The group phase lasts 25 minutes.

Points

Task completed with a workable schedule = 30 points.
Cheapest solution = 10 points.
Best utilization of crew (speed back to base, lowest number of layover days) = 10 points.
Failure to complete the task (ie produce a written solution) = -30 points.

Assessment/debrief

The process issues in the group discussion revolve around spotting the 'big picture', in this particular exercise providing a workable answer that meets legal requirements before getting into the detail of how to save money or get crews home quicker. The better candidates will spot this and keep the group focused on the task whilst setting out a broad aim at the start of the discussion. Weaker candidates will still contribute but mainly in the detail of what does or does not 'add up'. The weakest candidates will fail to contribute to either the task or the process, preferring to withdraw.

Shifting constraints

Alter some of the costings. For example, increase DXB to $60 or alter some of the legal requirements such as reducing crew duty time from 12 to 11 hours. Inform the group after 10 minutes.

A presentation would have to follow the group activity. 'Presentations' would, realistically, be the only competence that could be assessed. It can, however, be insightful to assess the processes used in the group discussion to 'nominate' a volunteer to deliver the presentation as part of 'Influence' or 'Interpersonal Skill', and also see how much support the volunteer is given by the other group members. The danger with this approach is clearly that only one candidate can be assessed under the 'Presentations' competence. Therefore, other candidates need to be given an opportunity to make a presentation, say by adding a presentation to each group activity if four or more activities are being used. Alternatively the presentation might not be formally assessed but used as an opportunity for a debrief, particularly in a development centre.

Sample wording for additional presentation task

At the end of the group phase, *one* member of the group should be in a position to present your solution including schedule and costs to the assessors in the form of a short, maximum five minutes, presentation using any appropriate visual aids.

Devising activities from scratch

A cynic might say that 'there is nothing new under the sun'! There is more than a grain of truth in the notion that most activities are 'old wine in new bottles', following well established formulae. However, this lack of uniqueness does not in itself make an activity any the less appropriate or effective. Whatever the type of activity you are devising, 'trial' it before using it in a real situation. Get colleagues to try it out or see if it can be used as part of assessor training or in a management development programme.

Group activities

Group activities broadly fall into two categories: open-ended and closed discussions.

Open ended discussions have no 'right' answer. The exercises in Chapter 11 are examples of open-ended discussions. Other well known examples of open-ended discussions include 'balloon debates', where the group has to decide the priority order for some kind of limited resource, for example for individuals to be rescued from a cave or to receive a kidney transplant. Each possible choice has a number of positive and negative aspects, for example the brilliant researcher on the verge of a breakthrough for a cancer vaccination, who has also been convicted of child abuse. This means that decisions are largely dependent on the values of the participants, making for no easy or obvious answer.

Closed activities have a clearly defined outcome or deliverable with 'right' and 'wrong' solutions. There may be more than one correct answer or solution, but the outcome is clearly objective rather than subjective. This may be the solution to a mentally-based problem-solving activity such as those in Chapter 13, or a more physically-based activity such as those in Chapter 12.

Another frequently used category of closed activity, not included in this book, is *rank-ordering exercises*. The best known of these types of exercise are NASA Moonwalk, Jungle Survival and Desert Survival. In the original concept, candidates are required to rank-order a number of items in terms of their importance, initially individually, and then as part of a group. These activities were designed as training exercises to illustrate the benefits of group consensus decision making. The candidates' original answers are compared with an 'expert' answer, which results in an 'objective' rating of the accuracy of their answers. However, they can also be used for assessment purposes, with or without the individual phase.

You can devise your own rank-ordering exercises. You will need an 'expert' answer. The sample below is based on information taken from Doganis (1991); it asks participants to rank the reasons people choose to fly on a particular airline. You might use a similar idea such as reasons customers choose your product. There are also more controversial contexts such as the addictive power of some drugs, or what people look for in a partner. The same format can be used to assess 'Planning and Organizing' when the items to be ranked are stages in a process such as managing a project. These can be tailored to a specific industry or sector.

Sample rank-ordering task

Reasons for choosing an airline

The task

Research conducted in Europe identified the following reasons for airline choice by passengers. The research was conducted by market researchers asking passengers, as they entered an airport, why they had chosen the airline they were about to travel on. The researchers would choose a mix of people: businessmen, families, holiday makers, different ages, etc. They were given a list and could choose more than one option.

Please order these according to which you think were most frequently mentioned by passengers. Use 1 for most frequently mentioned down to 11 for least mentioned. Do not award 'ties'. Try to think as widely as possible. Do not rely solely on your experience as a traveller. Your aim is to come to a 'better' score than the other team.

	Correct answer
Price	5
Convenient schedule	1
No choice	4
Aircraft type	9

Airport facilities	11
In-flight comfort (eg, seats)	7
Flight attendant/service	6
Loyalty to carrier	2
Frequent-flyer programme	10
Reputation for safety	3
On time arrival/departure	8

Task Time: 15 minutes

Points

'Best' score (ie, lowest overall score) = 20 points.
Second 'best' score (if applicable) = 10 points.
Score lower than 20 = 20 points.
Score lower than 30 = 10 points.
Failure to hand in to the assessor a written decision on the above table within 15 minutes = –20 points.

Managing the exercise

You would need to transfer the items to a table, obviously leaving out the correct scores. Scoring is the difference between the group answer and the 'correct answer'. Therefore, the lower the score the better or more accurate the answer. For example, if the group score item one, price, at 5 they would score 0. A group score of 1, on the other hand, would generate a score of 4 (5–1). All scores are plus; do not award minus scores irrespective of whether the group answer is higher or lower then the 'correct' answer. Do not get involved in a long debate about the accuracy of the group score! For assessment rather than development exercises, it is often easier to simply collect in the answer sheets and post the scores without giving the correct answer.

Which type of group activity is the most effective?

The potential disadvantage of many open-ended activities is that it can be relatively straightforward for seasoned candidates to 'play the game' and display the desired behaviours. It can be fairly easy for participants to temporarily abandon their true beliefs in order to create a harmonious atmosphere and not let their 'real' approach to conflict emerge.

A harder 'edge' can be added to these activities by allocating specific roles or stances to be taken, as in the 'Charity Allocation' activity in Chapter 11, where each participant is required to present the case for a specific charity as allocated by an assessor. The other activities in Chapter 11 are all split into individual and group phases. This enables a comparison to be made between individual and group decisions, which gives an indication of the degree to which a participant is prepared to change his or her view. This can form the basis for follow-up questions, at an interview, in a selection context, or in a debrief in a development centre.

In contrast, participants can often, despite themselves, become quite involved and 'lose themselves' in the task completion element of closed activities, particularly if at least three or four group activities are used in the process. The points aspect of many of the group activities in Chapters 12 and 13 also helps in adding to this atmosphere. As a result participants are more likely to let their guard down and display their 'true' approach. One psychologist, Jeremy Holt, writing in *People and Organisations @ Work,* published by the BPS, has even suggested that the popular TV series 'The Apprentice' is the 'next big thing in assessment'. He argues that one way to break the artificiality of candidate behaviour in many group activities would be, in the context of the activities in this book, to make success in the points scoring, in other words winning, key to selection in the role rather than just a 'fun' add on. A radical approach which perhaps risks losing some potentially skilled candidates but, as Holt suggests, this would bring out the 'real person'. Remember, if you took this option you would also have to alter the briefing notes for the activity.

The potential downside to some of these activities is that because of their low face validity they can seem irrelevant or even childish to some participants. Some might, for example, find building bridges from paper (in Chapter 2) somewhat demeaning or pointless. As we saw in Chapter 1, low face validity is really only a PR issue but, nonetheless, if this stops potentially good internal applicants from applying for a post it can be a barrier to effective recruitment and the credibility of the entire process.

Constructing group activities

Tasks need to 'build in' a number of elements. They need to give participants the opportunity to display one or more of the following skills.

See the 'big picture' and identify critical information

This is one key reason for the points system in some of the group activities. Do participants take into account how to score maximum points or
do they just concentrate on the task itself? For example, are points gained
for speed, and/or quality/accuracy? How can points be lost? This is critical in assessing 'Analytical Thinking'. It is also important in that it gives
all participants an equal opportunity to contribute to the activity. For
example, an activity such as 'Cash Register' (Chapter 13) could be criti-
cized for hinging solely on participants' ability to spot the difference
between fact and inference. The points system, however, still gives participants who are less knowledgeable in this area an opportunity to
contribute to the group's strategy: 'Should we resubmit?' or 'Should we
buy a clue?'

Use resources to accomplish a task

Activities should not require specialized or technical knowledge,
although it may be that one group member may have more to add than
others, as is the case in many workplace group situations. However, it is
not specialized knowledge that is being assessed. All the necessary
information should be provided in the activity and participants asked to
work only with that information. This also equally applies to individual
analytical exercises such as 'Transport Manager' (Chapter 10). In this
activity candidates with no knowledge of or interest in cars should not
be disadvantaged.

Work under time pressure

Tasks should be achievable in the time limit, but only if the group works
together effectively and with an appropriate sense of urgency.

Resolve differences

Tasks should be sufficiently complex or multi-dimensional so that no one answer or approach is immediately obvious. There should be a reasonable expectation that the task will generate different views and approaches from participants.

Share information to solve a problem

One well known technique for building this into an activity is a 'broken information' exercise. The best known example is the 'Zin Obelisk', the father of broken information exercises! In these activities participants are each given around five to six pieces of information on cards which, when combined (a total of around 30 pieces), provide through logical analysis the solution to a particular problem. The constraint is that participants are only allowed to share their information verbally. Examples in this book include 'Who Got The Job?' (Chapter 13) and 'Flight Roster' (Chapter 14). These activities are relatively straightforward to devise. For example, from 'Who Got The Job?':

> There were four assessors at the assessment centre.
> One assessor was from Singapore.
> Two assessors were from the UK.
> One assessor was Egyptian.
> The successful candidates were from different countries than the assessors.

Manage either multiple tasks or constraints on resources and approach

Role plays

In devising role plays keep the brief, well, brief! The role plays in Chapter 8 are typically no longer than a page and, in many cases, are only a short paragraph. In the stressful environment of a selection process it is important that participants are not bogged down with vast amounts of detail, turning the activity into more of a memory test than an assessment of skill. For the same reason, avoid giving names to the two role players in the brief. Their real names can be easily used.

As a general rule, the longer the brief the more time should be allocated for participants to prepare. This provides another reason for keeping the brief short as it cuts down on the preparation time, allowing more activities to be included in the assessment process. In a similar vein, keep the time for the actual meeting relatively short. In the role plays in Chapter 8, either 15 or 20 minutes has been allocated for the actual meeting depending on the complexity of the brief. Twenty minutes should be regarded as an *absolute maximum* for this type of activity.

In devising briefs, ask what the typical issues individuals in this particular role face in the working day. The role plays in the book take typical people-management issues faced by supervisory and first-line managers, such as giving feedback and career counselling.

In trays

In trays tend to have low face validity. The context can seem somewhat contrived: 'You are suddenly called away and have no deputy'. However, they can generate useful evidence to assess 'Planning and Organizing'. Whilst there does not need to be one right answer, overall the tasks in the in tray should lend themselves to being broadly categorized as high, medium or low in terms of importance, whilst all being urgent in terms of the time available. The in tray should also allow the participants the opportunity to give a rationale for their solution and say how they would approach each issue. Answers could be followed up either at an interview or, for development centres, a debrief.

Specific, departmentally-based, tasks

These types of exercise have the advantage that, if well constructed, they have high face validity. However, as we saw in Chapter 1, face validity is not always beneficial. It can mean candidates getting side-tracked into questioning the accuracy of the brief and, in some cases, needing a separate process for internal and external candidates.

To design these activities you will need the skills of the internal consultant. Effective questioning skills are needed to get the appropriate information from which to produce a brief. They are also essential for helping the client to clarify the key skills they want to assess. Try a question such as, 'If you could be a fly on the wall and watch the candidates in any one real work situation, what would it be?' Involvement of the line department is vital in order to both get information for the briefs and to then check on the accuracy and relevance of the exercise.

Below is an example of a role play and written report designed specifically to assess candidates for a role in management development. Competencies to be assessed might include 'Interpersonal Skill', 'Customer Service', 'Analytical Thinking' and 'Written Communication'.

Sample activity for management development role

TNA meeting and proposal

Trainer brief

You have been asked to see the head of a department. You have only been given brief details that she or he wants to talk to you about team-building and developing customer service.

You don't know the manager personally, having never met before, but have heard rumours that she or he can be quite 'pushy' and at times aggressive.

You have 20 minutes to conduct the meeting to gain as much information as possible to prepare a short *written proposal* to the manager on how you and he might move forward on the issues discussed.

You will have 10 minutes before the meeting to prepare your approach and questions.

You will have a *maximum* of 50 minutes after the meeting in which to write your proposal. You may present different options if you feel this is appropriate, but indicate clearly which would be your preferred option. We would also like you to outline what you feel are the strengths and possible weaknesses of your preferred proposal.

Role player brief

In general try to let the participant *lead and guide you* through the interview. Act neutrally towards the participant. The participant has been told that you have a reputation for being pushy and aggressive but do not display these behaviours in the interview. On the whole try *not* to volunteer information or ideas unless prompted to do so. You have your own ideas but want to hear other suggestions. Keep strictly to the allocated 20 minutes, claiming pressure of another appointment if the participant tries to overrun.

You run a section comprising five supervisors each with about 15 staff. Each section administers a range of HR functions for a designated number of departments as well as carrying out some cross-departmental specialist functions. If asked, some of the competencies for each role are: Supervisors – 'Leadership', 'Customer Service', 'Planning and Organizing', 'Influencing' but *not* 'Interpersonal Skill'. Other staff – 'Customer Service' and 'Interpersonal Skill'.

If asked, you can't remember specifically how each supervisor scored in his or her appraisal, although you think they all got graded as 'superior'. Promise to give the participant this information later, if pressed.

For some time now you have been concerned about a lack of communication between the different teams. They interpret policies differently and in your view give preference to work involving the departments they look after. You also get a feeling from informal feedback that some of the team are not customer-oriented, preferring to rigidly hide behind the rules and procedures. You organized a one-day customer workshop for all the team last year. You were too busy to attend personally. Although you heard good things about the course and the evaluation sheets were positive, things did not subsequently improve. You think that this is because the supervisors are generally afraid of giving negative feedback to their staff. Although you would not easily admit this if asked directly, you would not deny it.

Although you have not got any fixed ideas, you have heard excellent reports about a two-day outdoor team-building programme, and you also remember doing a course in your last company where everyone completed the Belbin Team Role Inventory. You feel it would be best if you *did not attend* any training programmes, claiming that this might intimidate the quieter members of the team.

Sample activity for departmental recommendation

Competencies assessed could include 'Written Communication', 'Analytical Thinking', 'Influencing' and 'Interpersonal Skill'. This type of activity has higher 'currency' if induction or initial training are generally perceived to be potential problem areas in the department in question. To ensure fairness, candidates would all have to be internal to the department.

Induction and initial staff training recommendations

Individual task

Your task is to produce a short *written* outline of what you feel are *two strengths and two potential areas for development* for induction or initial training in department X, with one recommendation for change. You may include any current aspect(s) of induction or initial training. Try to present as much detail as possible to back up your argument(s). You will have 20 minutes for this task.

Group task

As a group you have a total of 25 minutes to agree one discrete recommendation for change. You may choose one of the individual recommendations produced in the individual task phase, devise a hybrid, or come up with an entirely new recommendation.

One member of the team should be in a position to give a short, maximum three minutes, presentation of your proposal at the end of the group task. The assessors may ask questions after the presentation.

Some additional activities

Assessing performance feedback

This activity, generally the final exercise, requires participants to give each other feedback based solely on the activities in the assessment or development centre. Participants need to be paired together at the start of the process. In the case of an odd number of candidates, participant A would feedback to B, B to C, and C to A. In this activity 'Performance Feedback', 'Analytical Thinking' and 'Written Communication' could be assessed. In organizing groupings throughout the assessment centre, the feedback pairs must be kept together in order to be able to gather evidence for the feedback session. You will also need to provide participants with two additional sheets. The first is a list of the behaviour indicators for each competence they are assessing their colleagues against. The second is a short feedback form that only needs sections for comments and a rating, one for each competence.

The benefits of this activity are that it fairly accurately mirrors the real issues and tasks in giving feedback in the workplace, in other words it has high face validity. It can be stressful confronting performance issues with another colleague. In addition, participants have to match behaviours to an appropriate competence and use these to make an assessment. The other benefit is that new role play activities do not need to be created to assess 'Performance Feedback'; each feedback session will be unique.

Sample wording for activity to assess performance feedback

Performance feedback

Your final task will be to run a short feedback and coaching session with one of the other participants from the assessment centre.

At the start of the assessment centre you will be paired with one other colleague and, therefore, you'll need to collect evidence of her or his performance as you participate in the various activities. This person will also be collecting evidence in order to give you feedback. You will be given copies of any written work the person produces. There will be slots throughout the programme for you to review your evidence in preparation for the feedback session.

You will need to base your feedback on the following three competencies:

1. Oral Communication.
2. Interpersonal Skill.
3. Customer Service.

You will have 10 minutes to deliver your feedback.

After you have completed the feedback session you will be asked to complete a short feedback form and an overall rating of performance. You will have 20 minutes for this task.

Presentations

Typical topics for a supervisory/first-line management role might include issues and challenges facing the sector, organization or particular department. Some issues to consider when using presentations:

- Delivery and the content need to be assessed using separate competencies. Using the framework in Chapter 2, use 'Presentations' for delivery and 'Analytical Thinking' for content.

- If you are primarily interested in the content and ideas, why use a presentation at all? Ask yourself if the role requires the job-holder to make presentations or conduct group briefings. If not, it can be inappropriate to ask candidates to put forward their idea in a presentation. This adds unnecessary stress and can result in the content not being accurately assessed or negatively assessed because the presentation skills were poor, even though the actual ideas may have had considerable merit.

* Should candidates be allowed to pre-prepare presentations before the assessment centre? The answer to this depends on what exactly you are assessing. The competence of 'Presentation', as defined in the framework presented in Chapter 2, covers areas such as structure and visual aids as well as delivery. If you aim to assess all these aspects of presentation, then *do not* allow pre-preparation as there is no way to be sure who has structured the presentation or produced any visual aids. If you are only looking to assess delivery skills, then pre-preparation is appropriate. If you are allowing pre-preparation, make sure you have laptops with PowerPoint available.

What if I am not so creative?

Don't worry, you don't have to start from scratch! It is possible to generate activities by reworking some widely available tasks using an established formula. For example, broken information exercises can be easily made from the types of activity found in 'Puzzle Problem' books sold in newsagents. Try also to think of games and experiments as the basis for group exercises. For example, you could rework the egg drop experiment, where an egg has to be dropped from around 10 feet or three metres without breaking. The group is only given limited materials, such as tissue paper and paper clips, with which to protect the egg!

What's the future for assessments?

The current debate seems to be about the potential for computer-based testing. As is usually the case, opinion seems divided, with some suggesting that the rhetoric has not, to date, been backed by any significant application. Robert McHendry of psychology consultancy OPP, for example, states that the only example of a widely used computer-based work sample he knows is of the one used in the UK driving test! Others talk glowingly of the potential use of simulations such as audio simulations of phone calls and video clips of work-based scenarios that candidates have to respond to.

It may well be that the designs for the future need to lend themselves to online application, although these are expensive to design and their validity is, as yet, untested. Group activities are obviously difficult to apply online, whilst in trays and report-writing exercises seem to have more immediate potential. Role plays offer the possibility of growth but may restrict the range of participant responses.

Key tips

- Don't be sucked into spending vast amounts of time revising activities to make them specific to a particular department or section. Exercises based in a neutral context can be equally if not more powerful in generating evidence of skill.
- Keep activities short and to the point.
- You don't need to start completely from scratch with a blank sheet of paper if you need 'new' exercises. Adapt existing exercises by adding tasks or using a basic formula as your template.

7

Further Reading

This book is primarily a practical 'how to' guide. However, you may want to follow up and find out more about some of the more theoretical concepts that underpin the key messages in the book. Some suggestions for each chapter are included below.

1. Is effective selection art or science? The case for assessment centres

History of assessment centres

Woodruffe, C (2001) *Assessment Centres,* 3rd edn, CIPD, provides an overview.

Best practice guidelines

The British Psychological Society (BPS) guidelines, *Design, Implementation and Evaluation of Assessment and Development Centres: Best practice guidelines* are available to non-members from The Psychological Testing Centre (www.psytechtesting.org.uk; go to 'downloads'). You can also download from the Psytech website (www.psytech.co.uk).

Meta-analyses/predictors of job success

This is an area covered by a huge literature. Some of the better known studies are:

Barrick, M R and Mount, K M (1991) 'The big five personality dimensions and job-performance; a meta-analysis', *Personnel Psychology*, **44** (1) pp 1–26

Bertua, C, Anderson, N and Salgado, J (2005) 'The predictive validity of cognitive ability: A UK meta-analysis', *Journal of Occupational and Organisational Psychology*, **78** (3) pp 387–410

Hunter, J E and Hunter, R F (1984) 'Validity and utility of alternative predictors of job performance', *Psychological Bulletin*, **96**, pp 72–98

Schmidt, F E and Hunter, J E (1977) 'Development of a general solution to the problem of validity generalization', *Journal of Applied Psychology*, **62**, pp 529–40

Smith, M (1994) 'A theory of the validity of predictors in selection', *Journal of Occupational and Organizational Psychology*, **67**, pp 13–31

Adverse impact

Bobko, P, Roth, P L and Potosky, D (1999) 'Derivation and implications of a meta-analytic matrix incorporating cognitive ability alternative predictors and job performance', *Personnel Psychology*, **52** (3) pp 561–89

Ford, J K, Kraiger, K and Schechtman, S L (1986) 'Study of race effects in objective indexes and subjective evaluations of performance – a meta-analysis of performance criteria', *Psychological Bulletin*, **99** (3) pp 330–37

Woods, S (2006) 'Cognitive ability tests and unfairness against minority ethnic groups: Two practical ways to check for unfairness in selection', *Selection and Development Review*, 22 (2) pp 3–8

Does attitude drive behaviour?

Azjen, I and Fishbein, M (1977) 'Attitude-behaviour relations: a theoretical analysis and review of empirical research', *Psychological Bulletin*, 84, pp 888–918

Fishbein, M and Azjen, I (1975) *Belief, Attitude, Intention and Behaviour: An introduction to theory and research*, Addison-Wesley

Utility analysis

Cook, M (1988) *Personnel Selection and Productivity*, Wiley

Parkinson, M (2005) 'Is it worth it? How to put a figure on the benefits of selection', *Selection and Development Review*, 21 (6) pp 3–7

Schmidt, F L, Hunter, J E, McKenzie, R C and Muldrow, T W (1979) 'Impact of valid selection procedures on work force productivity', *Journal of Applied Psychology*, 64, pp 609–26

Emotional labour

Emotions have been a growth area for research in occupational psychology although much of the attention has centred on emotional intelligence. Emotional labour is a quite different concept and was coined in Hochschild's 1983 study of flight attendants, *The Managed Heart* (University of California Press).

Other summaries of research into emotions including emotional labour are:

Fineman, S (ed) (2000) *Emotions in Organizations*, Sage

Zerbe W J, Ashkanasay, N M and Hartel, C E J (2005/6) *Research on Emotion in Organizations*, Vols 1 and 2, Elsevier

2. What are we assessing? Developing a competence framework

Definitions of competence

Boyatzis, R E (1982) *The Competent Manager: A model for effective performance*, Wiley

Campbell, J, McCloy, R, Oppler, S and Sager, C (1993) 'A theory of performance', in (eds) W Schmitt and W Borman, *Personnel Selection in Organizations*, Jossey-Bass

Motowidlo, S J, Borman, W C and Schmit, M J (1997) 'A theory of individual differences in task and contextual performance', *Human Performance*, **10** (2) pp 71–83

Spencer, L M and Spencer, S M (1993) *Competence at Work*, Wiley

Issues around competencies

Fransella, F, Bell, R and Bannister, D (2003) *A Manual for Repertory Grid Technique*, 2nd edn, Wiley

Iles, P and Salaman, G (1995) 'Recruitment, selection and assessment', ch 8, pp 203–33 in (ed) J Storey, *Human Resource Management: A critical text*, Routledge (This also provides an excellent overview of how recruitment strategy can fit into broader HR strategy.)

Rankin, N (2004) '*The new prescription for performance: the eleventh competency benchmarking survey*', *Competency & Emotional Intelligence Journal*, Benchmarking Supplement, Reed Publishing

3. Designing and running an assessment centre

Order of activities

Bycio, P and Zoogah, B (2002) 'Exercise order and assessment centre performance', *Journal of Occupational and Organizational Psychology*, **75** (1) pp 109–14

The exercise effect

Gaugler, B B and Thornton, G C (1989) 'Number of assessment centre dimensions as a determinant of assessor accuracy', *Journal of Applied Psychology*, **74** (4) pp 611–18

Reilly, R R, Henry, S and Smither, J W (1990) 'An examination of the effects of using behaviour checklists on the construct validity of assessment centre dimensions', *Personnel Psychology*, **43** (1) pp 71–84

Briefing

Bywater, J, Martin, T and Long, M (2005) 'Just how important is the briefing given to participants in development centres?', *Selection and Development Review*, **21** (2) pp 6–11

4. Assessor skills

Improving inter-rater reliability through training

For a thorough review, see Woehr and Huffcutt (1994) 'Rater training for performance appraisal: A quantitative review', *Journal of Occupational and Organizational Psychology*, **67** (3) pp 189–205. Although primarily aimed at appraisal training, the key messages can also be applied to other forms of 'objective' assessment.

Coaching

This is another growth area with a huge literature.

The British Psychological Society (BPS) has formed a Coaching Psychology Special Group. Non-psychologists can join as affiliates. You can access the Group's website via the main BPS site (www.bps.org.uk). This contains useful contemporary articles.

Selection and Development Review has a special edition on coaching, August 2004, vol 20 (4).

Also try the CIPD website for news, articles and resources (www.cipd.co.uk).

Young, D (2005) 'Developing the business case for coaching: A methodology', *Selection and Development Review*, 21 (4) pp 3–9

Attribution theory

Heider, F (1958) *The Psychology of Interpersonal Relations,* Wiley

Nisbett, R E, Caputo, C, Legant, P and Maracek, J (1973) 'Behaviour as seen by the actor and as seen by the observer', *Journal of Personality and Social Psychology,* **27**, pp 154–64

Seligman, M E P (1975) *Helplessness: On depression, development and death,* Freeman

Psychological biases

Many of the studies were not specifically carried out using assessment centres as the context. However, the basic psychological processes are the same irrespective of the selection tool used.

Morgeson, F P and Campion, M A (1997) 'Social and cognitive sources of potential inaccuracy in job analysis', *Journal of Applied Psychology,* **82** (5) pp 627–55

Secord, P F (1958) 'Facial features and inference processes in interpersonal perception', in (eds) R Taguiri and L Petrullo, *Person Perception and Interpersonal Behaviour,* Stanford University Press

Vanvianen, A E M and Willemson, T M (1992) 'The employment interview – the role of sex stereotypes in the evaluation of male and female job applicants in the Netherlands', *Journal of Applied Social Psychology,* **22** (6) pp 471–91

Watkins, L M and Johnston, L (2000) 'Screening job applicants: The impact of physical attractiveness and application quality', *International Journal of Selection and Assessment,* **8** (2) pp 76–84

5. The role of psychometric instruments in assessment and development

The references to meta-analyses included under Chapter 1 are also highly relevant here.

Cultural aspects of personality

Daouk, L, Rust, R and McDowall, A (2005) 'Testing across languages and cultures; Challenges for the development and administration of tests in the internet era', *Selection and Development Review,* **21** (4) pp 11–14
McCrae, R R and Costa, P T (1997) 'Personality trait structure as a human universal', *American Psychologist,* **25** (5) pp 509–16
Tyler, G, Newcombe, P and Barrett, P (2005) 'The Chinese challenge to the Big 5', *Selection and Development Review,* **21** (6) pp 10–16

Online testing

The *ITC International Guidelines on Computer Based and Internet Delivered Testing* are available from either the International Test Commission (www.intestcom.org) or the Psychological Testing Centre (www.psychtesting.org.uk).

The ITC journal, *Testing International,* has a special issue on internet testing: Vol 12, No 1, 2002.

Level A and B training

Listing on the BPS register of competence, renewable annually at £20 currently, includes a subscription to six issues per year of the *Psychological Testing Selection and Development Review*. This contains a range of short articles that are, in the main, more accessible than journal articles, which are often aimed more at an academic, rather than a practitioner audience.

6. Adapting and devising activities

There is no particular theoretical basis for this section of the book. There are a number of guides for writing role plays and simulations, although these mainly concentrate on their use in training programmes. Try the CIPD website as a good starting point (www.cipd.co.uk).

Doganis, R (1991) *Flying off Course*, Routledge

Part II
Activities

8

Role Plays

Overview

These role plays have been designed to assess a number of typical issues faced by front-line managers. These include giving performance feedback, dealing with workplace disputes, counselling and career development issues, and influencing without formal authority.

Role play 6 differs from the others in that two participants can be assessed simultaneously.

You will need to source a suitable number of role players who can creatively and consistently take the part of the second role player brief.

Timings are suggestions only. Plus or minus five minutes should not be seen as too critical as long as each participant is given the same timescale for the meeting and overruns are not permitted.

Role play 1

1a. Participant brief

You work for a large hotel chain and are responsible for the front office check-in. You have received a complaint letter from a customer about one of your front-office staff who was allegedly 'rude and aggressive' after a mix-up over a cancelled booking.

Looking through the staff member's file you find:

- Just under five years in the company.
- Seventeen days sickness during the last 12 months. Always single days or two days together, no longer periods, although you haven't yet had the opportunity to bring this up with the staff member.
- One complaint, for rudeness, for which the staff member received a verbal warning 18 months ago. This was given by another manager; you have only been responsible for this staff member for the past 12 months.
- One recent failure on the internal promotion assessment centre, on the day prior to the complaint incident. This didn't surprise you as you felt this staff member was overly confident. When you had briefed him or her about the assessment process, he or she seemed anxious only to find out how to 'pass' rather than develop skills. You advised him or her to gain extra practice before attending the assessment.

Before the interview provide a short written outline of your objective(s) for the meeting and what issues you hope to cover.

After the interview provide a short written outline of:

1. What action you would recommend and why.

If you recommend any disciplinary action state which section of the disciplinary code would be most appropriate.

Disciplinary code

Verbal Warning	Where there is a minor infringement of rules or where conduct does not meet acceptable standards in a minor way.
Written Warning	If the offence is a more serious one, or if a minor offence recurs after a verbal warning.
Final Written Warning	If there is a failure to improve and the employee's work, conduct or omission is still unsatisfactory, or if the misconduct is sufficiently serious to warrant only a written warning but not to justify dismissal.
Dismissal	If the employee fails to reach prescribed standards following repeated warnings.

2. A letter you would subsequently write to the customer.

Timing

You will have:
15 minutes to prepare for the meeting.
20 minutes (strictly) to conduct the meeting and 20 minutes for the follow-up work (decision and letter).

1b. Role player brief

You are a front-office receptionist at a large hotel chain and have been with the company for just under five years. You have been called to see your manager regarding a complaint made about you by a customer at the check-in desk.

This customer was, in your view, very aggressive. When he attempted to check in late in the evening you found that his booking for a junior suite had been cancelled by his office. You could only offer him a regular room. He then became abusive and rude, demanding that you found him a suite and that he should not pay because of the inconvenience.

You are also angry that you failed the internal promotion assessment, although your manager had advised you to gain more practice. You feel that this decision was completely unfair. Your previous manager, who never liked you and even gave you a warning for an exaggerated customer complaint, was one of the assessors. One of the candidates who passed is widely known as being very lazy at work. You are now two years 'behind' some of the people who joined the hotel with you and you need to catch up quickly.

During the interview, try to be 'pleasant' and not openly aggressive. However, you feel you are not at fault in this case. You want to go back quickly for your promotion assessment centre and any kind of warning may delay this. Be quick to mention anything that will support your case or divert the meeting from the real issue, such as the bias of assessors or that you are the one with the real grievance. Be prepared to admit that you could have been perceived as irritated or momentarily angry at the check-in desk, but only if you feel the manager has done enough to win your trust. However, do not admit this initially and insist that your behaviour was justifiable in the circumstances. It is appropriate to be somewhat defensive, but respond if you feel the participant (as your manager) is using questioning, listening and empathy skills effectively.

Role play 1

Suggested competencies

Written Communication, Customer Service (Letter), Analytical Thinking (Decision), Interpersonal Skill, Performance Feedback (Meeting).

Managing the exercise

Make sure that the participant's objectives for the meeting are collected before the meeting. These can be used in a development centre debrief or to assess the degree to which the participant kept the meeting 'on track'. Do not allow the meeting to overrun.

Assessment/debrief

Look for the degree to which the participant probed the staff member and kept the meeting 'on track'. Did the participant rush to a quick decision or give her or himself thinking time? To what extent were the pre-stated meeting objectives appropriate and met? Appropriate objectives would include hearing the employee's version of events and not getting side-tracked into issues such as the assessment centre performance and other earlier complaints. Other issues to explore are the appropriateness of any action: dismissal and final warning are probably too extreme. The tone of the letter to the customer should be apologetic without being openly critical of the staff member.

Role play 2

2a. Participant brief

A staff member has made an appointment to see you to discuss the result of a recent assessment centre for promotion to supervisor. You know that this person had been a supervisor in his or her last company but, for personal reasons, needed to move location. She or he was therefore forced to take this current job, which has much less responsibility and a lower salary than the previous job. The assessor notes from the assessment centre suggest that this person did not prepare for the assessment, as scores were poor in all competencies. In previous casual conversations with this person you also have picked up the feeling that he or she feels that assessment centres are not an appropriate selection tool as they involve non-work-related 'games' and that assessors are biased towards certain candidates.

Timing

You have scheduled *15 minutes* for this meeting.

2b. Role player brief

You were a supervisor in your last company but, for personal reasons, needed to move location. You were, therefore, forced to take your current job, which has much less responsibility and a lower salary than in your previous job. You have recently failed an assessment centre for the role of supervisor and decide to talk through the result with your boss.

You did not do a lot of preparation for the assessment centre as you had passed these kinds of thing in your previous company and have a lot of experience. In the role play, try to be vague and difficult to pin down. You want to express how unfair you think the whole system is as it is about acting, not ability, and the 'games' have nothing to do with the real job. If the participant (as your boss) is directive and starts to move quickly to solutions about development activities without listening or showing empathy, be defensive ('yes but...') and try to move the conversation back to the system, your previous record, etc. Similarly, do not admit, unless 'pinned down' by specific questions, your lack of preparation. If the participant is assertive and moves the conversation on to future actions appropriately after listening to you, you should respond positively.

Role play 2

Suggested competencies

Interpersonal Skill, Influencing, Oral Communication.

Assessment/debrief

To what extent does the participant balance empathy and listening with a more assertive approach in clarifying the importance of preparation? Does the participant want to move inappropriately to 'solutions' in terms of what to do next, thereby perhaps giving the role player an unrealistic or overly positive view of the action needed for promotion?

Role play 3

3a. Participant brief

One of your team comes to see you. This person has now been in the company for just over 10 years. She or he was recently unsuccessful, for the second time, at an internal interview for promotion to supervisor. The interview was in another department and you weren't personally involved in the selection procedure. Generally this person's work is excellent, although you feel that his or her somewhat passive nature may let him or her down at interviews. However, you have not mentioned this at the annual review for fear of demotivating the person.

Timing

You have allowed *15 minutes* for this meeting.

3b. Role player brief

You have recently failed, for the second time, to be offered promotion to supervisor at an internal interview, but in another department. You know you get good appraisals from your supervisor but are beginning to feel frustrated as you can see lots of younger, ambitious, career-minded people coming up behind you. In fact you wonder whether you shouldn't just spend more time at home and forget about promotion. You decide to talk it through with your supervisor. You have not got any clear objective for the meeting; you mainly want the chance to vent your frustration and for someone to listen. If the participant (as your supervisor) starts to offer advice and move to a quick solution be somewhat defensive ('yes but...', 'that's a good idea but...') and ask for unrealistic guarantees ('If I do this will I get promoted?').

Role play 3

Suggested competencies

Interpersonal Skill, Influencing, Oral Communication, Performance Feedback.

Assessment/debrief

Does the participant act as an 'ear' and listen to the role player, or want to move inappropriately quickly to a decision and solution? Does the participant make unrealistic promises that she or he may be unable to deliver?

Role play 4

4a. Participant brief

One of your team comes to see you. He or she is a newly appointed supervisor, but has been with the company for several years. In your opinion this person is hard working, highly competent technically and a real asset to the company.

Timing

You have allowed *15 minutes* for the meeting.

4b. Role player brief

You are a new supervisor and finding the job difficult. Whilst you're OK on the technical side of the job and can solve any problems your team brings to you, it's the people side of things you find difficult. The more people you ask for advice the more confused you get. Should you be 'soft' or 'tough, 'friendly' or 'distant'? You're also finding extra pressure at home as you seem to spend increasing amounts of time at work. You decide to see your boss to talk it over. You really just want a supportive listener at this stage. Become defensive ('yes but...') if the participant (as your boss) moves inappropriately to giving advice on supervision or suggesting development activities. However, if you feel that the participant has allowed you the opportunity to express yourself, be open to practical suggestions.

Role play 4

Suggested competencies

Interpersonal Skill, Analytical Thinking (suggestions for development), Oral Communication.

Assessment/debrief

As in role play 3, does the participant act as an 'ear', listen to the role player and give him or her an opportunity to express concerns, or want to move inappropriately quickly to a decision and solution? Similarly, does the participant make unrealistic promises that she or he may be unable to deliver?

Role play 5

5a. Participant brief

A member of your team comes to see you. His or her performance is fine overall. Like everyone, she or he gets on better with some team members than others. You have not personally noticed any particular tensions within the team and you are reluctant to act on second-hand information from one person about another. You did this once some time ago and it created a very difficult situation.

Timing

You have *15 minutes* before another important appointment.

5b. Role player brief

You are having really strong arguments with a colleague. He or she has a tendency to 'wind you up' with comments about politics, your effectiveness, friends at work – anything. Although you would be reluctant to admit to this unless pinned down by the participant (as your manager) at times you do 'take the bait' and make inappropriate comments to this other person. But in your mind you would never have done this if the person had kept quiet in the first place. So far, this has not had a direct effect on your work but you decide to chat it through with your manager. You want the manager to move this person to another section. If this happened the problem would go away. Keep pressing this point, particularly if the participant seems hesitant or unsure.

Role play 5

Suggested competencies

Interpersonal Skill, Influencing, Creativity.

Assessment/debrief

Is the participant assertive with the role player in refusing to move the other person? Does the participant explore the role player's actions in trying to manage the situation, or simply accept the role player's perception? To what degree does the participant 'take over' the problem for the role player or push the issue back to him or her?

This role play may have some legal implications. In some countries, such as the UK, the employer has a legal 'duty of care' to employees. This means that if an employee raises, even informally, a grievance or complaint about a colleague the company is duty-bound to address the issue. This may take the form of further investigation rather than specific action, but the key point is that the employer may have to take the matter further despite the stated wishes of the complainant. However, unless participants would be expected to have this background knowledge, for example in assessing for an HR-based role, it is not appropriate to score participants negatively for not raising these legal issues.

Role play 6

6a. Line manager

You manage a department of 25 staff. You have just arranged an informal meeting with your HR manager.

One of your staff, Mrs B, age 43, has been off for six months. She has an extreme form of glandular fever (ME), which leaves her exhausted. As far as you know, there is no accurate way to know if or when she will be able to return to work. Her absence has caused a considerable delay on a key project she is leading. She has sent in a sick note from her doctor for a further one-month absence. Since she has exhausted her sick pay entitlement, you want the HR manager to visit her urgently to establish when she will return and, if that cannot be done, arrange for her employment to be terminated. Your real reason for wanting the termination is that you believe Mrs B is not the easiest person to get on with or is as 'up-to-date' as you would like. Unfortunately, because you have been very busy and Mrs B has rarely been at work, you have not talked to her about her skills and knowledge. There is nothing on her personal file to suggest there are problems in this area.

You have also obtained authorization from your boss to recruit an additional project manager. This will increase the number of project managers and is not a replacement for Mrs B. All advertising is controlled by the HR manager. You will need to get him or her to put advertisements in the press and trade journals. You *definitely* want to recruit someone from outside the company because you want 'new blood' and you really don't think anyone on your present team is currently ready for promotion.

Before the meeting you look quickly through the pending tray to see if there is anything else, and find a memo from the HR manager asking for two reports. These are: 1) the regular monthly training return, a simple list of which staff have attended formal training courses and any appropriate feedback or test scores; this has not been submitted for six months; and 2) a request from one of her or his staff, the safety officer, asking for information on your safety procedures. Both memos are at the bottom of the tray, and have not been actioned due to the pressure of work.

All the information you need to complete the discussion is contained in the brief. Please do not 'invent' extra facts.

Timing

You will have *20 minutes* for preparation and up to *20 minutes* for the meeting.

6b. HR manager

You are responsible for training, safety and staff welfare in several departments. Your priorities are to comply with all the safety legislation and catch up on a backlog of training. To make matters worse, next week you have to make 10 per cent of the staff in one department redundant.

A line manager wants to see you today. She or he is not involved in the redundancies.

Your safety officer has told you that this department is being unco-operative about preparing an analysis of safety procedures. The request for the procedures was made six weeks ago.

You want to chase the manager for his or her last four training returns, which she or he should do monthly. This is getting serious because you need to report to your SGM. If you do not get these returns by the end of the week you can expect a drastic cut in your training budget.

You want to get some of the redundant staff who are junior clerks/typists transferred to this department. Although this would put the department over budget for a short time, juniors are always coming and going. You want to get some in if you can.

Your assistant confirms that in this department a project manager, Mrs B, has been off sick for six months. You have not had time to investigate this further. Staff regulations state that after six months absence, staff will not be paid further. However, as long as they can provide sick notes from a doctor their jobs will be kept open for a period of up to two years. The disciplinary procedure states that staff can be terminated for poor performance (excluding sickness) after two formal written warnings have been issued and training to correct weaknesses has been offered.

The line manager has been given approval to recruit an additional project manager. This is *not* a replacement for Mrs B. However, the process for recruitment has not as yet been started. Company regulations state that all jobs must first be advertised internally.

All the information you need to complete the discussion is contained in the brief. Please do not 'invent' extra facts.

Timing

You will have *20 minutes* for preparation and up to *20 minutes* for the meeting.

Role play 6

Suggested competencies

Customer Service (Internal Customer), Analytical Thinking, Influencing, Adaptability.

Managing the exercise

This role play differs from the others in that both roles can be taken by participants (see Chapter 4). In these circumstances, if one participant 'dries up' it can be appropriate to allow a brief time out and restart the meeting to allow both participants the opportunity to display effective behaviours.

Immediately after the role play has been completed, ask each participant to provide his or her short written summary of the meeting, ie agreed future actions. This is a strictly individual task. Allow a maximum of 10 minutes for this. Make sure that each participant completes the written summary individually without consultation.

* Assessment/debrief

Use the written summary to see if the participants agree on future actions ('Planning and Organizing' competence). More effective participants will take some time to summarize each point during the meeting itself. Often, however, participants can have completely different views on what has been agreed.

For the line manager a key issue is how open and 'up front' to be about Mrs B. Presenting this as an issue solely about sickness could easily lead to the HR manager feeling manipulated when the 'real' issues emerge. The line manager may then be seen as politically 'clever' or manipulative. Being open builds trust and allows problem-based strategies to be used in resolving the Mrs B issue.

In this situation there is a temptation to link separate issues in a type of hard positional negotiation ('If you let me advertise externally I'll do your training returns'). Ultimately, however, this can lead again to feelings of manipulation. For the HR manager a reasonable objective, at least at this initial informal meeting, might be simply to listen to and understand the concerns of the line manager rather than trying to resolve each issue.

Role play 7

7a. Participant brief

You are a manager in a relatively small branch of a large banking corporation. You have arranged a 15-minute informal meeting with a staff member to discuss her or his performance.

She or he is 25 years old, recently married and has in the past year become a new parent. She or he was promoted to the position of cashiering supervisor 12 months ago, with a team of four cashiers. This promotion meant that she or he was transferred to another branch 40 minutes from home. Her or his previous branch was within walking distance. She or he has worked for the bank since leaving school at 16.

Recently her or his performance has given rise to some concern. She or he has taken 15 days sick leave in the past six months, never more than two days at a time, for headaches, colds and tiredness. Company regulations state that staff can take 15 days sickness on full pay. A doctor's certificate is only required for 3 plus days of continual sickness.

Although she or he seems to get on well with her or his own team, one or two of the other staff in the branch have complained to you informally about a 'difficult' attitude. In addition, a small number of customers have complained. In general this is about a lack of urgency in responding to issues. Only two customers have written officially, but a number of others have complained verbally to you or other people in the bank.

Her or his last appraisal from the manager in the previous branch was generally OK, not glowing, but no real areas for concern. However, privately this manager has talked to you about a lack of motivation and ambition. He also complained about her or him being difficult to get along with. He also said he was amazed about the promotion, not because of a lack of technical knowledge, but because of her or his attitude. Because she or he could be argumentative, the previous manager was unwilling to make an issue of these concerns at the annual appraisal.

You were not directly involved in this person's appointment, but still have to manage her or him on a day-to-day basis.

The company operates a competence-based performance management system. As a supervisor, this person's competencies include 'Leadership' and 'Customer Service'.

Timing

You will have *20 minutes* for preparation and up to *20 minutes* for the meeting.

7b. Role player brief

You are 25 years old, recently married, and in the last year have become a parent for the first time. You work for a large bank and were promoted to the position of cashiering supervisor 12 months ago, with a team of four cashiers. This promotion meant that you were transferred to another branch 40 minutes from your home. Your previous branch was within walking distance. You have worked for the bank since you left school at 16.

You have taken 15 days sick leave in the past six months, never more than two days at a time, for headaches, colds and tiredness.

Approach the meeting, initially, in a neutral manner. For example, say 'Everything is fine' if asked a general question. Do not give the participant (as your manager) easy openings. Be prepared to become defensive if not treated assertively or with appropriate rapport. For example, you have never been shown any customer complaints so can't comment other than to say there are some particularly unreasonable customers in this branch. Mention that the manager in your last branch had a personal bias against you, if this is raised. If the opinion of other staff is mentioned, ask to know who specifically has said what and say they should have the courage to address problems to you directly. If your illness is raised, say that you are within the HR regulations for sickness, that, overall, your sickness record has been excellent and that the new baby and extra travelling mean your energy level is lower than normal.

Timing

You will have *20 minutes* for preparation and up to *20 minutes* for the meeting.

Role play 7

Suggested competencies

Performance Feedback, Interpersonal Skill, Oral Communication.

Assessment/debrief

Does the participant follow the rules for effective feedback? Does she or he only talk about first-hand feedback and avoid second-hand information, for example from the previous manager? Does the participant get quickly to the point, particularly when the role player is reluctant to open up? Does the participant have a realistic objective for an initial meeting, for example to provide feedback and ask for an initial reaction, or want to move inappropriately and quickly to solutions?

9

In Trays

Overview

A key element in effective time management is demonstrating an understanding of the difference between tasks that are urgent and those that are important. Urgent tasks are always defined in terms of the time available. In these in trays, most tasks are urgent! Important tasks, on the other hand, are defined in terms of a number of possible factors:

- The critical elements of the job role.

- Safety or cost implications.

- The source of a request. A request that may not in itself be important can become so if it is made by a demanding CEO! Similarly, some people would only be able to concentrate on other tasks after, say, they had phoned home to find out why their partner had called. They need to remove uncertainty before tackling other tasks.

Of course, tasks can become both urgent and important. For these reasons no one correct answer has been provided for these in tray activities. Assess participants in terms of the degree to which they have coherently and consistently presented an appropriate rationale for their ordering. However, for each in tray some broad ideas of categorizing tasks are provided as a guide.

Times can be reduced to add extra pressure, say 10 minutes for in trays 1 and 2. For reliability this must be consistently applied across all participants. These in trays have in the main been kept simple and brief to gain information in as short a time as possible.

In tray 1

The task

It is 2 pm. You have just been into town for lunch with some relations. On your return, the following are waiting to be dealt with. You have a team of two assistants. One is on holiday and the other post is currently vacant:

A. Message from your CEO: 'Please phone as soon as possible.'
B. Written message: 'Mr Y (important commercial client) has been trying to get in touch – please phone back.'
C. Diary appointment: Regular section meeting at 2.30 pm.
D. Diary appointments: Interview of applicants X and Y for new post at 3.30 pm and 4.15 pm respectively.
E. Afternoon e-mails.
F. Message from HR: 'Can we have a pre-meeting before this afternoon's interviews? Please phone to arrange a time. Message timed 1 pm.' (You realize you haven't prepared for the interviews.)
G. Message from Finance: 'Please complete the questionnaire we sent you last week. We must have the information by 4 pm otherwise your extra requests will be denied.'
H. The phone rings.

Put the above into priority order, stating the action you would take and your reasons.

Timing

Task time: *15 minutes.*

In tray 1

Suggested competencies

Planning and Organizing, Written Communication, Creative Thinking.

Assessment/debrief

Least important: C and E.
Removing uncertainty (allows the task to be rated relatively high): A, B, H.
Relatively important: D, F (D and F are linked), G.

In tray 2

The task

You are the HR manager in a large company. It is 9 o'clock on a Thursday morning and you have just arrived at work. This is later than usual as you were caught in a traffic accident. You have an HR Officer who joined you two months ago and an admin assistant in your team. The following are waiting to be dealt with:

A. Meeting: This begins at 10 am. You are talking about a report you have written and circulated. This is the first item on the agenda (after Apologies and Minutes of the Previous Meeting). The meeting is scheduled to end at 1 pm but invariably overruns.

B. Message from your partner: 'Please phone me as soon as you get in – urgent.'

C. Written message: 'Can you see the General Manager.'

D. Written message: 'Please telephone David Jones at the *News* about an article he is writing for tomorrow's edition on the recent controversial sackings. Mobile number 1234567. (Message timed at 7.20).'

E. New e-mails.

F. An item on next year's revised budget is on this morning's meeting agenda. You said you would provide revised figures from your department. You have forgotten all about it! The figures will take you about 30 minutes to produce. No one else can compile them. The budget is item three on the agenda.

G. Appraisal interview booked with a member of the section for 2 pm. You have not had an opportunity to prepare for this due to other pressures. You've had to postpone this once already, at your request.

H. The phone rings.

Put the above into priority order, stating the action you would take and your reasons.

Timing

Task time: *15 minutes.*

In tray 2

Suggested competencies

Planning and Organizing, Written Communication, Creative Thinking.

Assessment/debrief

Least important: E.
Less urgent: D and G (if postponed).
Remove uncertainty: B, C, H.
More important: A and F.

In tray 3

The task

You are a cabin crew manager for an international airline. Your role involves:

■ managing a group of cabin crew, which includes conducting appraisals and handling work and personal problems;
■ recruitment of crew;
■ arranging crew for PR events;
■ working on a project team to make recommendations to improve the rostering system. The rostering section operates 24 hours per day.

Today is 18 May and the time is 12.15 pm (GMT). You are unexpectedly asked to go on a five-day overseas recruitment trip due to the sudden illness of a colleague. No other qualified member of the team is available. Recruiting requires a long day, often more than 12 hours of concentrated work.

You have 45 minutes before you must leave for the airport.

You have a mobile phone you can use in any country but *no* laptop. For security reasons staff are not permitted to access their work e-mail in non-secure locations (eg internet cafes). The airline you are travelling with does not provide an on-board phone system and in common with many other airlines does not yet allow mobiles to be used on board. Flight time to your destination is five hours.

Due to financial cutbacks you do not have a secretary working for you.

A. Message: 'Customer Complaints phoned. They have an irate Commercially Important Passenger (CIP) who has complained about the rudeness of one of your crew. They want you to investigate, find out her side of the story and get back to them by 1 pm. They have promised the CIP a response by 1.30 pm. The crew member arrived home from a long overnight trip this morning.'

B. Message from PR section: 'The press conference you have arranged two crew to attend for PR has been moved forward to the 23rd. The crew you selected are now both unavailable. Need two suitable crew.'

C. Message: 'Call X (senior crew member) in Hong Kong at the crew layover hotel.'

D. E-mail from Station Manager Hong Kong: 'One of the crew has been arrested by the police. I am liaising with them.'

E. Message: 'New crew called. She is distraught. Had an argument with a senior and is threatening to resign unless something is done.'

F. Message: 'Crew member wants you to sort out a problem. She has been marked absent but she claims she called in sick.'

G. E-mail from Rostering Project Team Leader: 'Thought your ideas were very good. Need to talk to you about how to include them in the presentation to senior management on the 22nd. Unfortunately if I can't get some more information we will have to go with the original recommendations.'

H. E-mail from colleague: 'As you know, Don is retiring after many years in the airline. Please arrange to record your video anecdote which we are compiling for him by the 23rd at the latest. Thanks.' Don is a close friend and has been your mentor for many years.

I. Crew waiting outside your office for annual review, scheduled for 11.45 pm. You are running late.

J. Crew waiting outside your office for annual review, scheduled for 12.15 pm.

K. Diary appointment. Meeting with graphic designer and printer to finalize the layout for your new recruitment brochure. Must be agreed today if the printer's deadline is to be met. The brochure is to feature in a high-profile recruitment drive to be launched next week. If the printer's deadline is not met the brochure will not be ready for the launch.

L. Diary appointments for 19th and 20th; three crew reviews per day.
M. Phone message: 'Please see me urgently' from Section Head.

Put the above into priority order, stating the action you would take and your reasons.

Timing

Task time: *30 minutes.*

In tray 3

Suggested competencies

Planning and Organizing, Written Communication, Creative Thinking, Customer Service.

Materials required

To add an element of realism to the activity, it is possible to present the items A to M individually as, for example, 'real' messages or e-mails.

Managing the exercise

In this longer In tray you might consider introducing some information at later points in the 30-minute timescale. For example, give out all items at the start of the activity with the exception of D (give after 15 minutes), H (after 20 minutes) and G (after 25 minutes).

Assessment/debrief

Least important: A (response would not necessarily need your input), H. More important: C and D are linked. Leave action to station manager. E: deal with quickly but no time for action. K: get proofs, maybe call from the airport.
Less urgent: B and G (can be done when manager arrives at destination), F, I, J and L (if postponed).
Remove uncertainty: M.

10

Analytical/Report Writing Activities

1. Crew scheduling

The task

You work for a dynamic Pacific Rim airline (RD) based in Hong Kong (HKG). The airline has been granted rights for a new route (RD742) shown below.

Your task is to devise a schedule showing how you would crew these flights effectively. Assume a crew of 15 cabin attendants. Devise the schedule for when the route is 'up and running', in other words you don't need to bother about positioning crew for the first flights in the initial days of operation. There are no crew sleeping/rest areas allocated on the aircraft.

Your aim is threefold:

1. To get crews back to base (HKG) as quickly as possible so they can be utilized on other flights. All crew live in HKG. No crew are permanently stationed away from base.

2. To get the maximum legally possible flying hours from crew.
3. To keep incidental costs and overheads to a minimum.

Legal requirements

■ Crew must not fly more than 12 hours at any one time (includes time on the ground). This is called duty time.
■ Duty time starts one hour before take off and ends 30 minutes after landing.
■ Deadheading (flying as a passenger but for work purposes, for example to get into position at another destination) counts as duty time.
■ Crew must have a minimum rest of 11 hours between flights.
■ Crew must have one complete day off at base (24 hours) every seven working days. Days away from base are counted as working days regardless of whether crew have actually flown.

NB. These requirements have been simplified to keep the activity short. Work only on the information as supplied rather than using any of your own additional knowledge.

Costs

Average accommodation and allowance costs (per night per crew member): BKK (Bangkok) $30, BOM (Mumbai) $60, DXB (Dubai) $50. Deadheading (flying crew from one station to another): free on RD, on another carrier $1,000 per total crew.

Timing

You have *45 minutes* to provide a clear written solution and costs and hand them to the assessor.

Route RD742

Departs HKG (Hong Kong) 14:10 Local time.

HKG – BKK (Bangkok). Flying time 3 hours.

BKK – BOM (Bombay /Mumbai). Flying time 4 ½ hours.

BOM – DXB (Dubai). Flying time 2 ½ hours.

DXB – BOM. Flying time 2 ½ hours.

BOM – BKK. Flying time 4 ½ hours.

BKK – HKG. Flying time 3 hours.

Arrives HKG 15:15 (next day) local time.

Leaves HKG on Mondays, Wednesdays, Thursdays and Sundays.

Assume one hour on the ground at all destinations.

Crew scheduling

Suggested competencies

Written Communication, Analytical Thinking.

Assessment/debrief

In terms of an actual answer, the simplest solution is for each crew to layover at BOM and have them operate BOM – DXB 'shuttles' on the next following flight (eg on Wednesday for the crew who leave HKG on Monday) before waiting for the next flight (Thursday in this example) and operating back to HKG. This would get each crew back to HKG within seven days.

It may be cheaper to layover crew in DXB and BKK, but crews departing on the Monday or Thursday are too late back in HKG (by one hour) to meet the requirement for one day off every seven. This would necessitate deadheading crew to BKK on another carrier to operate the BKK – HKG return leg on Monday and Thursday (am). The DXB – BKK operating crew would also need to deadhead back from BKK – HKG after one night's rest on another carrier. This would mean total deadheading costs of $4,000, which eats into any savings made by the cheaper layover costs in BKK and DXB.

Crew scheduling possible solution

Crew leaves HKG	Nights in BOM (Outward)	Nights in BOM (Return)
Monday	2	1
Wednesday	1	3
Thursday	3	1
Sunday	1	2
TOTAL	7	7

Total: 14 nights in BOM × 15 crew × $60 = $12,600 (per week).

There is little advantage in deadheading in this scenario as other carriers would have to be used, although this would get crews back to HKG sooner.

2. Accommodation allocation

The task

You are an Accommodation Officer for South England University responsible for arranging room allocation in the university's halls of residence for mature students.

Fourteen non-UK students are arriving next week to start their courses. You have seven student units allocated for all of them. Each unit includes one double bedroom, a bathroom and access to a shared kitchen. Smoking is allowed in the units if both occupants agree. You may assume each student is single, studying for a first degree, and a non-smoker unless otherwise stated.

Who would you allocate to live with whom? Provide a list of pairings with a brief reasoning behind your choices.

Timing

Task time: *20 minutes.*

Non-UK students requiring accommodation

STUDENT	SEX	AGE	NATIONALITY	SUBJECT	OTHER
David	M	33	Australian	Biochemistry	Smoker
Suresh	M	22	Indian	Computing	
Emiko	F	28	Japanese	Psychology	
Ai Hua	F	29	Chinese	International Business	
Rita	F	40	Norwegian	Art	Married with 2 young children
Mohammed	M	23	Pakistani	Computing	
Dietter	M	24	German	English Literature	Smoker
Sophie	F	21	Swedish	Medicine	Unmarried mother of a small baby being looked after by her family in Sweden
Ellie	F	36	Greek	History	Member of feminist group in Athens
Fatima	F	22	Turkish	Dentistry	Devout Muslim
Gazi	M	30	Tunisian	Business	Spent six months in jail for assault
Kim	M	27	Singaporean	Business	'Born again' Christian
Bassam	M	21	Lebanese	Sociology	Asthma sufferer
Philippe	M	41	French	Maths PhD	Non-smoker

Accommodation allocation

Suggested competencies

Written Communication, Analytical Thinking.

Assessment/debrief

There is no one right answer to this activity. When working only with written profiles there is a risk of basing decisions on stereotypical judgements. However, more effective answers will base allocation on the explicit use of criteria such as:

- sex;
- cultural/national background;
- subject studied/interests.

3. Transport manager

Phase 1. Informal report

You are responsible for the purchase, maintenance and repair of the fleet of cars used by your company's regional sales staff. It has been decided to renew the fleet of cars.

The fleet currently consists of five Smith 'M' and seven Smith 'E' cars. The latter are used by the junior sales staff while the other cars are used by the senior sales staff.

Due to availability of certain models your choice is limited to the models listed in the table below.

Local garages offer a special discount for the purchase of cars, which is worth 5 per cent off the prices quoted if a *minimum of six from the same manufacturer but not necessarily the same model* are ordered. The garage supplying Smith cars also offers a loyalty bonus of a further 2.5 per cent discount on Smith models if at least six are purchased.

The Head of Sales has given you a report concerning the feelings of the sales team about the cars. The junior sales staff find that their car is too small for their general use. The lack of space is particularly noticed when exhibition display materials are carried, as happens at least four times a year. A capacity of 11 cubic feet for carrying materials is the necessary minimum. They also think their car is underpowered. However, this car has generally performed well with reasonably low maintenance costs and with a good record of reliability.

The senior sales staff, while liking the carrying capacity of their cars (any less space would be unacceptable), have found the driving position uncomfortable on long journeys. They also think that the car is not sufficiently imposing. Their status requires a more up-market car.

The report from the garage where the main servicing and repair of fleet cars is carried out states that the senior sales staff cars have been unacceptably costly to maintain and have had a high number of break-downs. However, over the years that the firm has been using these cars, a sizeable stock of spare parts has been accumulated in the garage stores.

You have a budget allowance of $310,000 maximum to buy 12 new cars. As the business is experiencing some cutbacks you would like your proposal to come in as far under budget as possible. You would also like the cars chosen to be as economical as possible to run and maintain.

You have to write a short report to your boss (Head of Procurement) outlining your choice of vehicles and the reasons behind your choice. You may decide on any combination of cars. Please use only the information contained in the following table to make your decision. Do not introduce any information you may already have about cars. You may assume all cars are four-door.

Timing

You have *50 minutes* to write your report.

Available cars

Car	Engine capacity (higher = more powerful)	Miles per gallon (urban)	Boot capacity (cu ft)	Price ($) before any discount	Other information
Smith M	1.8	28.1	13.0	28,000	Smith is an iconic US car manufacturer
Smith E	1.3	31.6	10.3	20,000	
Zidane 1	2.0	26.1	13.2	26,000	Zidane is an established French company
Zidane 2	1.6	22.1	10.6	18,000	Reports in the motor press suggest the interior is uncomfortable
Nakamura AB	1.3	21.3	11.1	25,000	Nakamur is a 'middle of the road' Japanese company
Nakamura CD	2.0	21.3	14.2	34,000	*Which Car* 'Comfort Car of the Year'
Sun Park C	2.3	28.1	Ample	35,000	Estate Car from Korean producer
Sun Park Z	1.6	24.8	11.3	25,000	
Clarkson X	2.5	23.2	Ample	35,000	4 x 4. Clarkson is an older UK manufacturer
Ballack 2	3.0	17.4	10.5	38,000	Ballack is known for its up-market cars. Which Car 'Style Car of the Year'
Lendl 3	1.8	32.5	12.5	20,000	Lendl is an Eastern European Company once known for the poor quality of its cars although current product meets contemporary criteria
Technik 9	2.0	23.3	13.3	36,000	Technik is a European Manufacturer known for its reliability and safety features

Phase 2. Presentation

Your boss has asked you to present your recommendations to a small panel of senior managers. You have been given 10 minutes preparation time and a maximum total delivery time of 10 minutes. As this is a last-minute request you will *not* be expected to prepare a sophisticated PowerPoint presentation, although a flipchart and whiteboard will be available for any supporting visual aids you wish to use.

Timing

You have a total of *20 minutes.*

Transport manager

Suggested competencies

Phase 1: Written Communication, Analytical Thinking, Customer Service.
Phase 2: Presentations, Influencing.

Materials required

Flipchart, whiteboard and pens.

Managing the exercise

Phase 2 is optional. In phase 2 use the assessor panel as the 'audience'. Do not allow other candidates to listen to presentations as this may lead to accusations that later candidates could learn from others' mistakes. Use a random selection method to decide the order of presentations. Keep strictly to timings: indicate to candidates when they are at the nine-minute mark, allow one minute overrun then stop the presentation as tactfully as possible.

Assessment/debrief

This is another exercise where there is more than one correct answer. Several combinations are possible. Effective answers will address the following key issues:

- Does the car chosen for the junior sales people provide enough boot space and power? Zidane 2 and Nakamura AB don't meet at least one of these criteria. The Lendl 3 meets the criteria and is also economical in terms of both running costs and purchase.

- Does the car chosen for the senior executives meet the required boot capacity (13 cubic feet or more) as well as the power and 'status' requirements. Technik 9, Nakamura CD, Zidane 1, Sun Park C and Clarkson X all meet the boot capacity and power criteria. Status and comfort issues are more difficult to objectively assess. The Ballack does not have a large enough boot.

- Has the candidate taken advantage of bulk purchase discounts for six or more cars from the same manufacturer? If not, is a good rationale given?

- Does the overall cost fall within the budget limit? Are issues of fuel economy mentioned?

11

Open-ended Group Decision Making

Overview

It is relatively easy for well versed participants to 'play the game' and be more accommodating than they would be in reality in open-ended discussions. To counter this, these exercises (with the exception of activity 3, Charity Allocation) include a written individual phase to gauge the degree to which participants have changed from their original view. Debriefs can be used to gather further information about the reasons for changes, if appropriate.

1. Redundancy

You work for XYZ airlines as a cabin crew manager. Due to poor business performance you have been asked to make some crew members redundant. There has been an initial call for volunteers, but that has been exhausted so compulsory redundancy is now the only option. Redundancy is *not* termination, in other words losing your job because of poor performance or a disciplinary issue. It occurs because of a reduction in the size of a business.

You have been asked to decide the order in which six crew should be made redundant, with number one as the first to be made redundant and six the last. You should allocate a different number to each person, so you cannot list two crew as, say, equal three.

XYZ is based in an emerging nation with no labour protection laws. Therefore the principles that often guide redundancy such as 'first in last out' do not apply here.

Company policy states that redundant staff will be given one week's salary for each year of service.

Redundant staff will be given preference for any vacant ground positions, but only if they have the necessary qualifications and experience.

Timing

Phase 1. Individual preparation

You will have *10 minutes* to make your individual decision. You should not discuss this decision with any other participants. You should record your decision on the attached sheet although you do not need to give reasons at this stage.

Phase 2. Group decision

As a group you will have *20 minutes* to agree your list and record this on the attached sheet.

Crew

A. Male, Sri Lankan, 28, six years' service. His wife was, until recently, also a cabin crew member but has left the job as she is expecting a baby. Good record on board but can clash with some managers in the department.

B. Female, Filipina, 26, two years' service. Trained nurse. Single. Has large family at home who depend on her income. Good performance and attendance record.

C. Male, British, 29, five years' service. Recently divorced. Has received several awards for improvement suggestions and handling emergencies. Attendance record has been poor for the past few months. Most of his work experience has been as cabin crew.

D. Female, Egyptian, 30, seven years' service. Former model now married to senior company manager. Poor attendance record. Regarded as poor at customer service. Features prominently in the current 'Face of XYZ' advertising campaign.

E. Female, South African, 29, less than six months' service. Single. Gave up a well paid job as a sales executive to join the airline. Achieved top mark in initial training. Speaks four languages fluently.

F. Male, Australian, 42, 15 years' service. Generally regarded as 'lazy' with a poor performance and attendance record. Married with three children.

Redundancy decision sheet

Crew Member	Individual Decision	Group Decision
A		
B		
C		
D		
E		
F		

Redundancy

Suggested competencies

Influence, Initiative, Interpersonal Skill.

Managing the exercise

At the end of the group phase collect the decision sheet.

Assessment/debrief

Use the decision sheet to see the extent to which participants may have changed their decision whilst under pressure. When combined with observations of participants' behaviour in the discussion, this can give helpful evidence of Interpersonal Skill and/or Influencing.

If the activity is being used as part of a development centre, this can be a good starting point for a verbal debrief, asking participants why they changed their views.

2. Delegation

The task

You are a manager in the loan applications department of a finance company. You are qualified and experienced in dealing with loan applications. You have a team of four including:

A – your deputy, who is fully qualified and trained but has been with the company for only four months.

B – 42 years old. Been with the company and in her current position for 14 years. Shows no inclination for promotion. Reliable and steady worker.

C – 22 years old. New graduate. Keen to develop and move on. One year in the role.

D – 33 years old. Transferred from another section six months ago as part of a reorganization. Was not happy about the move and seems demotivated, although previous reports indicated good skills and knowledge.

It is Monday, the start of the working week. For family reasons you suddenly have to take four days off, starting tomorrow. Looking at your diary, you have 10 tasks scheduled for the coming week. In the time you have available today you will only be able to complete two of the tasks yourself in addition to briefing the staff on the tasks you decide to delegate.

For each of the tasks, decide who in your team would be the most appropriate to delegate the task to (specify A, B, C or D) and which you should carry out yourself (S = Self). Please give a brief reason for your choice. Each task must be allocated to only one person: tasks cannot be shared between two or more team members. It is not possible to leave a task until the following week.

Delegation involves the manager giving to a junior team member the responsibility, but not the accountability, for carrying out a task. If it is carried out effectively, matching the appropriate task to the appropriate person, this can be highly motivational. On the other hand, it can be seen as 'dumping' if the task is not sufficiently challenging.

Timing

Phase 1. Individual preparation

You will have *15 minutes* to provide your individual written decision and reasoning on the attached sheet.

Phase 2. Group decision

As a group you will have *15 minutes* to agree your decision and record it on the attached sheet.

The 10 tasks

1. Attending the monthly managers meeting. This decides budgets, application of company policy, personnel issues, etc and takes place on Wednesdays.
2. Filling in the monthly overtime returns for accounts.
3. Working out the summer holiday roster.
4. Providing information to a features journalist writing a piece on loans. Hopefully the company can get some good publicity from this.
5. One of the team (D) has been having a lot of sick days recently. The issue needs to be addressed directly with this person.
6. Interview panel for a new team member on Thursday.
7. Informal meeting about improving customer service standards with a training consultant. Time to be arranged.
8. Showing a group of new starters around the section at 4 pm today and explaining the role of the department. Total time one hour.
9. Briefing the team on a new procedure.
10. Making the final decision on three problem applications.

Delegation decision sheet

Task	Individual Decision (A–D or S) and Reasoning	Group Decision
1		
2		
3		
4		
5		
6		
7		
8		
9		
10		

Delegation

Suggested competencies

Analytical Thinking (Individual Phase), Influencing, Initiative.

Assessment/debrief

Only assess Analytical Thinking from the decision made in the individual phase of the exercise. Whilst there is no one correct answer there are some fairly obvious pitfalls to avoid:

- Tasks 1 and 6 must be delegated because of scheduled times.

- Task 5, for reasons of confidentiality, should be kept by the manager. It probably makes sense for the manager to carry out task 9 to save time rather than briefing one member of the team to brief the others.

- Are tasks distributed evenly amongst the team rather than with over-reliance on the deputy (A)? Tasks 2, 3, 8 and possibly 4 and 6 could be appropriate to delegate to one of the team *other than* the deputy.

3. Charity allocation

The task

You represent a well known charity (the assessor will tell you which one). You have been asked to attend a meeting to decide the allocation of a bequest made by a wealthy philanthropist. He has donated $1 million for charitable purposes. He has indicated the charities he would like to be considered for the bequest. However, he has also made a clear condition that the money cannot be shared amongst all the charities: at most the money can be divided between two of the nominated charities. This is to take advantage of a tax loophole.

The meeting is scheduled to last 30 minutes, by which time a decision must be made otherwise the money will be kept on deposit for 10 years. The trustees have allocated each representative two minutes at the start of the meeting to put forward the case for his or her charity. The trustees have also indicated that they will not accept any decision based on a 'lucky draw', as legal experts have advised them that this may lead to future challenges to the bequest.

All information is taken from the websites of the various charities.

Timing

You will have *five minutes* to prepare your initial case to the group. The group discussion will last *30 minutes*.

Amnesty International

'Amnesty International is a worldwide movement of people who campaign for human rights. Our work is based on careful research and on the standards agreed by the international community. We are independent of any government, political ideology, economic interest or religion.

Amnesty International mobilizes volunteer activists – people who give freely of their time and energy in solidarity with those whose rights have been abused. At the latest count, there were more than 1.8 million members, supporters and subscribers in over 150 countries and territories in every region of the world. We come from all walks of life, with widely different political and religious views, united by our determination to work for a world where everyone enjoys human rights.'

Greenpeace

'Greenpeace is an independent non-profit global campaigning organization that uses non-violent, creative confrontation to expose global environmental problems and their causes. We research the solutions and alternatives to help provide a path for a green and peaceful future.

Greenpeace's goal is to ensure the ability of the earth to nurture life in all its diversity.

Greenpeace organizes public campaigns:

- for the protection of oceans and ancient forests;
- for the phasing-out of fossil fuels and the promotion of renewable energies in order to stop climate change;
- for the elimination of toxic chemicals;
- against the release of genetically modified organisms into nature;
- for nuclear disarmament and an end to nuclear contamination.

Greenpeace does not solicit or accept funding from governments, corporations or political parties. Greenpeace neither seeks nor accepts donations which could compromise its independence, aims, objectives or integrity. Greenpeace relies on the voluntary donations of individual supporters, and on grant-support from foundations.

Greenpeace is committed to the principles of non-violence, political independence and internationalism. In exposing threats to the environment and in working to find solutions, Greenpeace has no permanent allies or enemies.'

Oxfam

Oxfam uses a range of approaches to achieve change and improve people's lives, including saving lives through emergency response; longer-term development programmes; and campaigning to achieve lasting change.

Through our global campaigns we are using the energy and commitment of people all over the world to end poverty. We work with people in over 70 countries around the world, campaigning to achieve lasting change.

Oxfam's work spans issues including trade, conflict, education, debt/aid, health, HIV/AIDS, gender inequality, climate change, democracy and human rights, conflict and natural disasters.'

Cancer Research UK

'Cancer Research UK is the world's leading charity dedicated to research on the causes, treatment and prevention of cancer.

Our vision is to conquer cancer through world-class research, aiming to control the disease within two generations.

We support the work of over 3,000 scientists, doctors and nurses working across the UK. Our annual scientific spend is more than £213 million, which is raised almost entirely through public donations.'

RSPCA

'The objectives of the Royal Society for the Prevention of Cruelty to Animals are to:

- prevent cruelty to animals by enforcing the existing laws;
- amend legislation as is necessary for the protection of animals;
- sustain an intelligent public opinion regarding animal welfare;
- take whatsoever steps are necessary to educate the community with regard to the humane treatment of animals;
- diffuse information about the care, protection and treatment of animals by publishing and circulating literature and conducting lectures, seminars and competitions;
- conduct, manage, operate or encourage clinics, hospitals, homes or shelters for the care, treatment, maintenance and protection of animals, and to acquire and conduct ambulance and/or other means of relevant animal transport.

The objectives of the Society are implemented by the RSPCA Inspectors, who are the Society's uniformed representatives. The Inspectorate are specifically trained in the area of animal welfare and in the enforcement of prevention of cruelty to animal legislation.

Inspectors investigate complaints of cruelty and neglect each year. Reports of cruelty cover many areas, including farm animals, companion animals, pet animals and native animals.

RSPCA believes that man must treat animals humanely. Where man makes use of animals or interferes with their habitat, he should bestow a level of care befitting man's own dignity as a rational, intelligent, compassionate being, and a level of care merited by the nature of the animal as a sentient creature capable of responding to man's care and attention. Such care should be marked by sympathy, consideration, compassion and tenderness towards animals.'

NSPCC

'The NSPCC (National Society for the Prevention of Cruelty to Children) is the UK's leading charity specializing in child protection and the prevention of cruelty to children. We have been directly involved in protecting children and campaigning on their behalf since 1884.

Our work to end cruelty to children includes:

- 180 community-based teams and projects throughout England, Wales and Northern Ireland.

- A free, 24-hour Child Protection Helpline that provides information, advice and counselling to anyone concerned about a child's safety. We also run a bilingual Welsh helpline, an Asian helpline in five Asian languages, and a textphone service for people who are deaf or hard of hearing.

- Public education campaigns, to increase understanding about child abuse and provide advice and support on positive parenting.

- Parliamentary campaigning to persuade Parliament and opinion-formers to put children's issues at the top of the political agenda.

- Child protection training and advice for organizations involved in the care, protection and education of children. For example, local and health authorities, sports bodies and young people's groups.

- Research into the nature and effects of child abuse.'

Campaign to Protect Rural England (CPRE)

'We are people who care passionately about our countryside and campaign for it to be protected and enhanced for the benefit of everyone. The countryside is one of England's most important resources but its beauty, tranquillity and diversity are threatened in many different ways.

We are a registered charity with about 60,000 members and supporters. They live in cities and towns as well as villages and the countryside. Anyone who supports our aims is encouraged to join. We operate as a network with over 200 district groups, a branch in every county, a group in every region and a national office, making CPRE a powerful combination of effective local action and strong national campaigning.

We are one of the longest established and most respected environmental groups, influencing policy and raising awareness ever since we were founded in 1926.'

Charity allocation

Suggested competencies

Influencing, Creativity, Oral Communication, Initiative.

Managing the exercise

Use a random selection method when allocating charities to participants (draw names from a hat) rather than giving participants a choice. You can either give the information on all the charities to each participant or restrict the sheet for a particular charity to the participant who will be 'representing' that organization. The latter method means that participants will have to prepare their case 'blind', not knowing anything about the other 'bidders'. This makes the task a little more challenging. You may want to substitute some of the more UK-based charities with international organizations or ones from other countries.

Assessment/debrief

In a development centre debrief there may be some defensiveness by participants about having to speak on behalf of a charity they may, in reality, have no particular support for, particularly if they feel they have not done well in the group discussion. In general it is not advisable to open up a long debate about this, although it may be worth mentioning that there are many occasions in work situations where managers need to be seen to support and implement policies and regulations they may not necessarily fully agree with.

4. Selection centre

The task

You are a member of a selection panel to the position of Recruitment Officer. Six candidates have attended an assessment centre and interview. You have to select one candidate only for the position. You cannot select more than one candidate and no other vacancies are expected for the rest of the year. The candidates have varied strengths and weaknesses against the required competencies, which are shown below.

All competencies are regarded as core to the role. There is no formal policy stating that a particular minimum rating must be reached in each competence before an individual can be appointed. This is left to the discretion of the assessor panel.

As a selection panel you must determine who is the best candidate to hire, based on the competency strengths and measures you as a panel have determined through the assessment programme.

Timing

You will have *10 minutes* for your individual decision and *20 minutes* for the group discussion.

Candidate information

Candidate	A	B	C	D	E	F
Years of relevant experience	10	2	15	1	4	5
Membership of professional body	No	No	Yes	No	Yes	Yes
Written communication	3	4	2	5	3	5
Planning and organizing	4	4	5	2	3	3
Analytical thinking	3	3	5	4	3	2
Customer service	2	4	5	3	3	5
Initiative	5	2	2	3	3	5
Interpersonal skill	3	2	4	3	3	3

Ratings are out of 5: 1 = No evidence; 2 = Not effective; 3 = Some skill shown but needs to be developed; 4 = Effective; 5 = Outstanding.

Selection centre decision sheet

Individual Decision	Group Decision
Candidate:	Candidate:
Reasoning	Reasoning:

Selection centre

Suggested competencies

Influence, Interpersonal Skill, Initiative.

Assessment/debrief

More effective groups will usually spend some time agreeing criteria for selection, for example whether there is a minimum acceptable rating that must be achieved, or a weighted scoring system, before moving to discuss each candidate.

12

Physical Task Group Activities

General introduction to group exercises in Chapters 12, 13 and 14

The group exercises in Chapters 12, 13 and 14 are largely designed to be run as 'fun' competitions between two or more groups. If a number of these exercises are used, this can often assist in creating an atmosphere where participants more readily let down their guard rather than actively managing their behaviour. It also allows participants to display some of the Planning and Organizing behaviours if they are able to link their suggestions to the points allocation.

Participants should not be rated according to the group's success in gaining points as this could lead to the 'exercise effect' (see Chapter 3). Care must be taken throughout to link observations to the specific competencies being assessed.

The exercises in Chapters 12, 13 and 14 contain an *optional* element termed 'shifting constraints'. These are alterations to some of the basic instructions contained in the activities. They are designed to throw a 'spanner in the works' and see how the group reacts to last-minute changes. You may be able to add some of your own shifting constraints. To ensure reliability in the process, shifting constraints need to be used in either all or none of the group activities in any one assessment process. Shifting constraints are particularly useful if 'Leadership' or 'Adaptability' is being assessed.

1. Construction tender

The task

You work for a construction firm that has been invited to tender to build a new residential complex. You are competing against other contractors to satisfy the client's needs for cost, speed, safety and space. The task is divided into two phases: planning and construction.

In the planning phase you must design a building from one sheet of A4 paper. The building must be closed at the top (have a roof) and have four connecting walls. It must be constructed from only *one* sheet of paper. Two sheets cannot be combined, neither can two buildings be made from one piece of paper. You are allowed to cut or score the paper but cannot use fixings (eg, glue, pins, staples).

Timing

The planning phase will last *20 minutes*. During this phase, if you want to use scissors or paper you will have to purchase them. Rulers and pencils are provided free.

The construction phase lasts five minutes. During this time you will construct as many buildings as possible. All materials including paper are free during this phase.

Points

Largest number of buildings constructed during the construction phase = 10 points.
Tallest individual building built during construction phase = 10 points.
Fastest construction of 15 buildings = 10 points.
Accurate written 'budget' of costings produced at the end of the planning phase = 10 points.
Failing 'safety' test (resistance to light wind) = -2 points each building.

NB. 'Unsafe' buildings do not count as part of your final total.

Costs

Each piece of paper = -4 points.
Use of scissors (each period of five minutes) = -4 points.
Costs only apply during the planning phase.

Construction tender

Suggested competencies

Creative Thinking, Interpersonal Skill, Planning and Organizing, Adaptability (if shifting constraints used), Leadership (if a leader is designated), otherwise Initiative.

Materials required

Rulers (one per team), scissors (one per team), paper, pens, pencils.

Managing the exercise

Ask for the costings immediately after the end of the planning phase. Do not allow time for a participant to write them up; they should be available at the end of the planning phase. Make sure they are 'accurate' and note when you have given materials, if applicable. Also make sure to keep a record of each five-minute period during which scissors have been allocated. Wind resistance requires blowing gently on each 'building'!

Assessment/debrief

In the planning phase look for the following themes:

- How does the group divide time? More effective groups allow some time to rehearse the actual construction rather than spending all the time debating the design.

- How well organized is the group? Does someone take care of the 'budget' and hand it in on time (this is an easy way to gain 10 points). Does someone keep track of the time?

- Does the group discuss some of the big picture issues: priority/strategy for speed versus height; how much to 'spend' on resources in the planning phase?

Shifting constraints

This concept is explained in detail in Chapter 4. Choose only *one constraint.* After 10 minutes increase the costs for each type of material to −10 points each; or after 15 minutes increase the points for the tallest building to 30 points; or after 15 minutes reduce the construction phase to three minutes.

2. Bridge building

The task

Your task is to build a bridge using only the materials provided for the purpose (one ream of A4 paper and a stapler). The bridge must span a gap of six feet between two tables. It must not be supported in any way other than by resting on the tables. It must not be fixed to the tables in any way nor be below the surface level of the tables at any point of its structure. The bridge should be constructed from unprocessed materials. This does not preclude trying out designs or making prototypes in the design phase.

Timing

You have *20 minutes* to design your bridge and your production process. At the end of this design phase you will have a maximum of six minutes to construct your bridge.

Points

Completion of the task within six minutes = 25 points.
Fastest completion = 15 points.
Failure to complete the task successfully = -15 points.

Bridge building

Suggested competencies

Planning and Organizing, Interpersonal Skill, Creativity, Adaptability (if shifting constraints used), Leadership (if a leader is designated), otherwise Initiative.

Materials required

Staplers, staples and A4 paper.

Assessment/debrief

In this activity the more effective teams make sure that they spend some time rehearsing their production process. In this sense Planning and Organizing is a critical competence as it is easy to spend most of the planning time in trying to agree a design and not discuss the fastest way to actually build the bridge.

Shifting constraints

Reduce planning time to 16 minutes (give after 10 minutes); or increase the space from six to eight feet (give after 10 minutes).

3. River crossing

The task

Your task is to get all the team members across a small (12 feet) 'river' as quickly as possible using only the coloured paper to act as stepping stones. You will have two large stepping stones (blue) and two small stones (red). Once a stone has been placed in the river it cannot subsequently be moved.

Team members have to step from one stone to another; jumping is not allowed. If one team member 'falls in', in other words touches the floor with his or her foot, the entire team has to start the exercise from scratch but the stones must stay in their position.

In addition, the team has to transport a box of precious cargo which must always be held by two of the team once the crossing commences. When the crossing commences, no verbal communication is allowed. If the team has to start the exercise again because a member 'falls into' the river verbal communication is allowed until the crossing restarts.

Timing

Total task time = *20 minutes.*

Points

Successful completion of the activity in the time limit = 40 points.
Verbal communication during the crossing = -10 points each time.
Quickest crossing = 30 points.
'Falling off', feet touching the floor = -10 points.
Cargo not being held by two people = -5 points per 30 second period.

River crossing

Suggested competencies

Planning and Organizing, Creativity, Adaptability (if shifting constraints used), Leadership (if a leader is designated), otherwise Initiative.

Materials required

Per team: two A2 sheets of paper with a blue cross and two A4 sheets of paper marked with a red cross. Small heavy object to be the 'cargo' (brick or dumbbell).

Managing the exercise

Look for teams breaking the rules. For example, the cargo not being always held by two people or talking during the crossing, but don't tell the participants at the time. Simply present the number of penalty points at the end. If the group 'falls off' you will need to instruct them to start again if they do not do this voluntarily. Mark out a 'river' with pieces of masking tape.

Assessment/ debrief

Look for the degree to which the team rushes to action rather than planning an approach.

Shifting constraints

Double each of the penalty (minus) points; or the group can purchase an extra red stone at -20 points. Both are given after eight minutes.

13

Mental Task Group Activities

Overview

Please refer to the general introduction to group activities at the start of Chapter 12.

1. Letter cards

The task

An assessor will give a set of cards to your group. Each card will bear a letter. Your task is to use up all the cards in making complete words. Each card can only be used once. Proper nouns (eg names of people, cities or products) and hyphenated words (eg pre-judge) are not accepted. When the assessor calls 'finish', only words displayed using the cards will be accepted. Verbal answer or answers written on a separate sheet will not be accepted.

Timing

Round 1: 14 cards   (8 minutes)
Round 2: 18 cards   (5 minutes)
Round 3: 21 cards   (3 minutes)

Points

Each card left unused = -2 points per card.
Each word of two or three letters = 2 points each.
Each word of four or five letters = 4 points each.
Each word of six or seven letters = 6 points each.
Any word of eight or more letters = 10 points each.

Each incorrect spelling (assessor's ruling is final) = -10 (the cards are counted as 'unused' and scored as such).

Letter cards

Suggested competencies

Planning and Organizing, Interpersonal Ability, Creativity, Adaptability (if shifting constraints used), Leadership (if a leader is designated), otherwise Initiative.

Materials required

The following letters stuck on index cards: C, D, H, N (x 2), P, Q, R, S, T (x 2), X, U, (x 2), E (x 5), I (x 2).

Assessment/debrief

To what extent does the group agree an approach or plan, for example dividing tasks with somebody looking for longer word(s)? Or does the approach resemble a 'free for all' with each person working independently?

Shifting constraints

Shorten the timings. For example, make rounds 2 and 3 four and one minute long respectively; tell the participants just before round 2. Alter the scores, for example in round 3, make the penalty for any unused letter -15 points.

2. Cash register

The task

Based on the following story, the group has to decide whether the statements are true (T), false (F) or you can't say definitely without getting some extra information (?).

Timing

Within 15 minutes give your team's written answer to the assessor. At the end of the first 15 minutes the assessor will give you back your overall score (five points for each correct answer). The assessor will not, however, tell you which answers were right or wrong, or the other team's score.

You will then have a further 10 minutes to:

Decide if you wish to submit a revised answer sheet.
Revise your answer sheet if you wish to resubmit different answers.

Points

Each correct answer in the initial submission = 5 points.
Not re-submitting (does not apply if you have all answers correct) = -10 points.
Each previously incorrect answer now corrected = 10 points per answer.
Each previously correct answer now incorrect = -5 points per answer.

The story

A businessman had just turned off the lights in the store when a man appeared and demanded money. The owner opened a cash register. The contents of the cash register were scooped up and the man sped away. A member of the police force was notified promptly.

The statements

1. A man appeared after the owner had turned off his store lights.   T   F   ?

2. The robber was a man.   T   F   ?

3. The man did not demand money.   T   F   ?

4. The man who opened the cash register was the owner.   T   F   ?

5. The store owner scooped up the contents of the cash register and ran away. T   F   ?

6. Someone opened a cash register.   T   F   ?

7. After the man who demanded the money scooped up the contents of the cash register, he ran away.   T   F   ?

8. While the cash register contained money, the story does not state how much.   T   F   ?

9. The robber demanded money of the owner.   T   F   ?

10. The story concerns a series of events in which only three persons are referred to: the owner of the store, a man who demanded money, and a member of the police force.   T   F   ?

11. The following events in the story are true: someone demanded money, a cash register was opened, its contents were scooped up, and a man dashed out of the store.   T   F   ?

Cash register first submission (answer sheet A)

1. A man appeared after the owner had turned off his store lights.   T   F   ?

2. The robber was a man.   T   F   ?

3. The man did not demand money.   T   F   ?

4. The man who opened the cash register was the owner.   T   F   ?

5. The store owner scooped up the contents of the cash register   T   F   ?
    and ran away.

6. Someone opened a cash register.   T   F   ?

7. After the man who demanded the money scooped up the   T   F   ?
    contents of the cash register, he ran away.

8. While the cash register contained money, the story does not   T   F   ?
    state how much.

9. The robber demanded money of the owner.   T   F   ?

10. The story concerns a series of events in which only three   T   F   ?
    persons are referred to: the owner of the store, a man who
    demanded money, and a member of the police force.

11. The following events in the story are true: someone demanded   T   F   ?
    money, a cash register was opened, its contents were scooped
    up, and a man dashed out of the store.

Cash register resubmission (answer sheet B)

1.	A man appeared after the owner had turned off his store lights.	T	F	?
2.	The robber was a man.	T	F	?
3.	The man did not demand money.	T	F	?
4.	The man who opened the cash register was the owner.	T	F	?
5.	The store owner scooped up the contents of the cash register and ran away.	T	F	?
6.	Someone opened a cash register.	T	F	?
7.	After the man who demanded the money scooped up the contents of the cash register, he ran away.	T	F	?
8.	While the cash register contained money, the story does not state how much.	T	F	?
9.	The robber demanded money of the owner.	T	F	?
10.	The story concerns a series of events in which only three persons are referred to: the owner of the store, a man who demanded money, and a member of the police force.	T	F	?
11.	The following events in the story are true: someone demanded money, a cash register was opened, its contents were scooped up, and a man dashed out of the store.	T	F	?

Cash register

Suggested competencies

Analytical Thinking, Oral Communication, Adaptability (if shifting constraints used), Leadership (if a leader is designated), otherwise Initiative.

Managing the exercise

The answer to the puzzle is: all statements are '?' except 3 which is 'F' and 6 which is 'T'. The businessman who turned off the store lights is not necessarily the owner of this specific store. The person who demanded money is not necessarily a robber; he could be a creditor, for example.

We don't know *for sure* who opened the cash resister, who scooped up the contents, or what the cash register contained. 'Dashing out of the store' and 'speeding away' are not necessarily the same.

Give scores verbally and do not give any extra information as to where errors have been made. If one group scores full marks, the exercise continues with other groups. If one group submits their answer before the 15-minute deadline, wait until the time is completed before giving their score. If all groups have submitted their answers you may give out the scores before the 15-minute deadline.

Failure to submit *written* answers within 15 minutes results in a zero score. Do *not* allow verbal answers.

Assessment/debrief

This exercise is based on a well known activity to spot the difference between fact and inference. As such it often gives candidates an opportunity to display some of the Analytical Thinking behaviour indicators. However, be careful not to negatively assess candidates who do not contribute to the fact/inference debate. They can display other positive behaviours in terms of keeping the group on track and communicating effectively.

Shifting constraints

At the end of 15 minutes you must still give your answer to the assessor. However, the assessor will not now give you back your score. The rest of the activity continues as per original instructions; or task time is cut to five minutes for the second phase; or after the first submission you can buy a clue in the form of a question at -15 points. Possible clues: 'Think about who demands money and why', 'Is a business always owned by a man?'

3. Programme planning

The task

You are the Controller of Programmes for Channel 1 TV in the former communist state of Belugistan. Your task is to plan the Channel 1 programme schedule. Your main rival is the Channel 2 TV network. Both channels rely on government financial support in addition to advertising revenue for survival. However, the government has announced that with the rise of satellite TV it can only afford to support one station in the future. It will continue to support the company with the best audience ratings.

Channel 2 has planned its own schedule well in advance and can be seen on the Programming Master Plan. You should plan Channel 1's schedule bearing in mind the strengths and weaknesses of Channel 2's schedule. Refer also to 'Programme planning' (below) to guide you. Your aim is to pull in as large an audience for the evening's viewing as you possibly can, given the programmes at your disposal. The programme alternatives you have are limited, and can be seen on the programme cards held by your team members. The programmes already slotted in to your schedule *cannot* be moved (eg 9 pm news). You should write in the programmes you decide to use on the Programme Master Plan.

Timing

Task time: *25 minutes.*

Programme planning: some criteria

■ Channel loyalty. If the audience switches on to your channel to begin with, they are likely to stay with you for the rest of the evening. (Peak viewing period is from 7 pm to 10 pm.)

■ Inheritance factor. Following a very popular show, a high proportion of the audience will stay to watch the next show, not out of choice, but simply because it is on.

■ Pre-echo. An audience will tend to watch part of a programme on the same channel *preceding* the main programme they wish to see that evening.

■ Pre-scheduling. An attempt to schedule a big audience-puller a few minutes earlier than the opposition.

Points

Accurate programming (timings add up) = 15 points.
Fastest accurate completion = 10 points.
Accurate completion under 15 minutes = 15 points.
Inaccurate programming (ie timings don't add up) = -20 points.
Failure to produce schedule on the master plan within 20 minutes = -30 points.

Programme master plan Wednesday evening

	CHANNEL 1	CHANNEL 2
5.45	International News and Weather	
6.00	'Today': Magazine programme with local news	
6.35		Australian Soap Opera
6.45		
7.00		MTV Rock Show
7.30		UK Soap Opera
8.00		Seinfeld, US Comedy
8.30		The Sopranos, US Drama
9.00	News	
9.25		
9.30		News
10.00		International Soccer
10.45	Current Affairs Programme	
10.50		Film Awards Ceremony

Programme planning

Suggested competencies

Planning and Organizing, Influencing, Adaptability (if shifting constraints used), Leadership (if a leader is designated), otherwise Initiative.

Materials required

The following programme information pasted on to individual index cards:

SPORTSWORLD
Horse Racing
Soccer Highlights
Tennis
Time: 45–60 minutes. There is room for manoeuvre here. A segment could be cut, saving 15 minutes if necessary.

SHORT SEGMENTS
Three short segments films are available. You may use any number of them, or none at all if you wish.
1. Tom and Jerry cartoon (five minutes)
2. Johnny Bravo cartoon (five minutes)
3. Travel Shorts – five destinations (five minutes each)

ARTS PROGRAMME
A documentary on the career of U2 (repeat)
Time: 65 minutes.

JAWS
Classic hit film from the 1970s. A killer shark terrorizes a US holiday resort.
Time: 90 minutes.

FRIENDS
American comedy series. The one where Joey fails the audition.
Time: 30 minutes.

THE BILL
Police drama serial.
Time: 30 minutes per episode. Two episodes can be shown back-to-back.

Assessment/debrief

In this activity speed of completion gains the most points. Do the team members work this out or do they spend an inappropriate amount of time discussing the specifics of the schedule? The information on programme planning is largely a 'red herring' given the points structure. This activity is therefore a particularly strong vehicle for assessing Planning and Organizing indicators.

Shifting constraints

Task time is now 20 minutes; or points for the fastest completion are now 40; or you now cannot use the 'Sportsworld' programme. Each to be given after 10 minutes.

4. Broadcast appeal

The task

Your task is to produce a short radio 'infomercial' advertising either your:

- company;
- department, to the rest of your company; or
- favourite charity.

The infomercial should include some music, and at least half of your team (a minimum of two people) must speak in the commercial. The commercial must not include any silences of longer than three seconds.

Timing

The infomercial must be ready to 'air' after 20 minutes of production and rehearsal time. After 15 minutes the 'producer' will want to know the exact time, between 30 and 90 seconds, that your infomercial will run for. You should give him or her a written note of the predicted time as soon as you have decide this and in *no case after* 15 minutes. Failure to give a written estimate to the producer will result in the assumption that your infomercial will last for 90 seconds.

Points

Within 5 seconds of the predicted time = 25 points.
Each team member over the minimum of half of the team who speaks = 10 points per team member.
More than 10 seconds deviation from the predicted time = -25 points.

Broadcast appeal

Suggested competencies

Influence, Creativity, Planning and Organizing, Adaptability (if shifting constraints used), Leadership (if a leader is designated), otherwise Initiative.

Materials required

A stopwatch is essential.

Assessment/debrief

As no points are awarded for creativity, those who take the big picture view tend to quickly agree a script and spend most of the time in 'rehearsal' to gain the maximum number of points.

Shifting constraints

Minimum time for infomercial is now 45 seconds (given after 10 minutes); or *every* team member now has to speak on the infomercial (given after 14 minutes).

5. Who got the job?

You work in cabin crew recruitment for a large international airline. A number of candidates have attended an assessment centre. From the clues given to your team, work out which candidate(s) were successful (letter, age and nationality). Solutions must be *written* clearly. Verbal solutions are not acceptable. The assessor will only tell you if the answer is accurate or not. No further information or guidance will be provided. You may then present an amended answer if your initial answer is inaccurate.

Team members will each be allocated different clues. They may read out their clues but not physically pass or show them to other group members.

Timing

Task time: *20 minutes.*

Points

Correct solution = 25 points.
Fastest correct solution = 15 points.
Correct solution under 15 minutes = 15 points.
Incorrect solution = -30 points each time.
Breaking a rule (showing clues) = -5 points each time.

Who got the job?

Suggested competencies

Interpersonal Skill, Planning and Organizing, Adaptability (if shifting constraints used), Leadership (if a leader is designated), otherwise Initiative.

Materials required

The following clues cut out and each placed on individual index cards:

Eight candidates attended the assessment centre.
Candidate A is Sri Lankan.
Candidate B is Jordanian.
Candidate C is Indian.
Candidate D is a Filipina.
Candidate E is a Filipina.
Candidate F is British.
Candidate G is Egyptian.
Candidate H is Singaporean.
Two males were unsuccessful.
One female was successful.
Filipina always refers to a female.
The results were unfortunate for one candidate because his flatmate was not successful.
There were three male candidates.
The Jordanian shares a flat with the oldest person at the assessment centre.
The oldest candidate was successful.
There was a maximum age difference of six years between the candidates.
The youngest candidate is 24 years old.
Candidate C is the youngest.
Candidate C is male.
Unfortunately the youngest candidate was not successful.

There were four assessors at the assessment centre.

One assessor was from Singapore.

Two assessors were from the UK.

One assessor was Egyptian.

The successful candidates were from different countries than the assessors.

Candidate E is two years younger than the candidate from the same country.

Candidate D is three years younger than the eldest candidate.

Candidate H is 25.

One successful candidate is 25.

Managing the exercise

Distribute the clue cards randomly amongst the group. If the group provides an incorrect answer, simply say 'The solution is incorrect.' Do not give any further information even if pressed. If any candidate breaks a rule (eg passing cards) do not inform the group but make a written note to deduct five points for each infringement. The group must be allowed to regulate itself without guidance.

The answer is: two were selected – one Sri Lankan male (A, aged 30) and one female (Filipina E, aged 25).

Assessment/debrief

To what degree do any of the participants raise the issue of accuracy versus speed? How does the group react if they offer an incorrect solution?

Shifting constraints

After 15 minutes change the scores to 35 for correct solution and -40 for an incorrect solution; or after 13 minutes remove the penalty for breaking the rules.

14

Supplementary Group Activities

Overview

These activities adopt the themes and structures of activities in Chapters 11, 12 and 13. They have been included as potential extra exercises if other exercises become 'over-exposed' or if there is a need to regularly run several group exercises with a nominated leader.

Activity 1, 'Committee on anti-social behaviour' is a potential additional exercise for Chapter 11 (Open-ended group discussion); 2 'Paper castle' for Chapter 12 (Physical task group activities) and 3 'Word groups' and 4 'Flight roster' for Chapter 13 (Mental task group activities).

Please also refer to the general introduction to group activities at the start of Chapter 12.

1. Committee on anti-social behaviour

You are a member of a project group convened by the government to look into the problems of late-night drunken behaviour in city centres. In order to decide on which measures should be taken to combat this, a trial city has been chosen so that ideas may be tried out there.

Individual phase

Look at the following suggestions and use the attached sheet to decide which you think would be the most, and least, effective and practical. Put one by the suggestion you think would be most effective down to eight for the least effective. Do not award ties, for example two number threes; each suggestion must have a separate rating. You will have 10 minutes for this task.

Group phase

The group will then have 15 minutes to agree a decision.

Suggestions

A. Public houses should have restricted opening hours.

B. Supermarket sales of alcohol should be limited to two hours per day.

C. Ration cards should be issued to limit the amount of alcohol each person can consume each week.

D. The drinking age should be raised to 21 and identity cards issued as proof of age.

E. An 'alcohol education' programme should be set up for all local schools.

F. The price of all alcoholic drinks should be increased and the extra money spent on a general publicity campaign to warn against the dangers of alcohol.

G. Police resources should be increased to crack down on under age drinkers and those found drunk and disorderly.

H. Courts should increase punishments for drunken behaviour.

Timing

You will be given *25 minutes*: 10 for the individual phase and 15 for the group phase.

Committee on anti-social behaviour decision sheet

Suggestion	Individual Choice	Group Choice
A		
B		
C		
D		
E		
F		
G		
H		

Committee on anti-social behaviour

Suggested competencies

Influencing, Oral Communication, Creativity.

Assessment/debrief

Use the decision sheet to see the extent to which participants may have changed their decision whilst under pressure. When combined with observations of participants' behaviour in the discussion, this can give helpful evidence of Interpersonal Skill and/or Influencing. If the activity is being used as part of a development centre, this can be a good starting point for a verbal debrief, asking participants why they changed their views.

2. Paper castle

The task

The group should build a free-standing, self-supporting structure that must be at least 35 centimetres high from the floor level, and have a base of at least 2 × 2 feet. The structure may not be attached to, or supported by, anything other than the paper supplied.

Timing

You will be given 20 minutes to plan and design. However, any paper used during this time will be charged at -5 points per sheet. At the end of the planning/designing stage, you will have three minutes to build your castle. You will be charged -1 point per sheet of paper used.

One of your team should provide the assessor with a *written* record of the number of sheets used, at both planning and construction phases, at the end of the activity.

Points

The highest castle = 30 points.
For every six inches over the required height = 20 points.
Successfully completing the entire task = 40 points.
Failure to provide an accurate written record after three minutes of construction = -15 points.

Paper castle

Suggested competencies

Interpersonal Skill, Creativity, Planning and Organizing, Adaptability (if shifting constraints used), Leadership (if a leader is designated), otherwise Initiative.

Materials required

A4-size paper, rulers.

Managing the exercise

Measurements are deliberately presented in both metric and imperial measures.

Assessment/debrief

A key issue to look for is the extent to which the team has agreed and practised an efficient production process before the construction phase.

Shifting constraints

Bonus points are now awarded for each three (not six) inches over the minimum height, communicated to participants after 15 minutes; or the highest castle is now + 40 points, also communicated after 15 minutes.

3. Word groups

The task

The group has 36 cards which should be arranged into groups of three words, all with some connection. This could be a common subject, sound or theme. The assessor will decide if each grouping is acceptable.

Timing

The activity is divided into three phases. Phase one will last 10 minutes, phase two four minutes and phase three two minutes. In phases two and three, points will be awarded only for new groups where at least one word is changed from a previous grouping.

Points

Each group of three (assessor's decision is final) = 3 points.
Fastest completion of the phase with all cards correctly used = 20 points per phase.
Each unacceptable grouping = -3 points.

Word groups

Suggested competencies

Interpersonal Skill, Planning and Organizing, Adaptability (if shifting constraints used), Leadership (if a leader is designated), otherwise Initiative.

Materials required

Stopwatch.
The following words stuck on individual index cards:

GOLD SILVER BRONZE
TURKEY SPAIN FRANCE
DIAMOND CLUB SPADE
MARS SATURN JUPITER
ORANGE BLUE YELLOW
PLUM PEAR PEACH
SOAR GLIDE FLY
FINGER HAND ARM
CHICKEN LAMB BEEF
CENTIMETRES METRES KILOMETRES
TEE BEE FEE
MARATHON 10,000 METRES 100 METRES

These are the 'obvious' groupings but many other creative options are possible, for example Gold, Blue and Plum (colours)!

Managing the exercise

Ensure that there is consistency in determining whether a grouping is acceptable. Be flexible and creative!

Assessment/debrief

The task in this exercise is relatively straightforward. The key is if the group realizes that they can gain extra points for speed, and act accordingly whilst still being accurate.

Shifting constraints

After five minutes increase the points for unused cards to -10 each; or reduce the task time to eight minutes (give after five minutes).

4. Flight roster

The task

You work in scheduling for a large airline with a base in the Middle East. Your task is to determine the work roster for one of the crew (Ms X) at the Middle East base for the first seven days of the month. You may assume Monday is the 1st. Only use the information on the cards. Do not assume extra information.

Please give your *written* answer to the assessor including flights, accurate flight numbers, specific days and days off. The assessor will only tell you if the answer is accurate or not. No further information or guidance will be provided. You may then present an amended answer if your initial answer is inaccurate.

You may share the information on your cards but not physically show your cards to anyone else.

Timing

Task time: *25 minutes.*

Points

Correct solution = 25 points.
Fastest correct solution = 15 points.
Correct solution in under 20 minutes = 15 points.
Incorrect solution = -30 points each time.
Breaking a rule (showing clues) = -5 points each time.

Flight roster

Suggested competencies

Interpersonal Skill, Planning and Organizing, Analytical Thinking, Adaptability (if shifting constraints used), Leadership (if a leader is designated), otherwise Initiative.

Materials required

The clues should be cut out and placed on index cards:

Y is X's best friend.

Y is going on leave on the 3rd immediately after she returns from a trip that morning.

Y is flying to London Heathrow on the 1st.

X is flying with her best friend on one trip.

X's roster has completely different destinations to her flatmate's.

A is X's flatmate.

A's boyfriend is from Egypt.

A's boyfriend's family moved to Jordan recently.

X has bid for a Sydney trip this roster.

A is flying to Sydney this roster.

A has flights to Manchester and London Gatwick.

A has flights to Delhi and Chennai in India.

After her only night stop away from base in the first week, X has 22 hours rest before her next flight.

X has one UK trip in this period, arriving back at base in the morning.

X has two turnaround flights in this period.

X has no African flights in this period.

After her trip to India, X has two days off.

X has one Middle East flight in this period.

X's flatmate's boyfriend has asked her to post a letter to his family as she is flying to where they live.

One of X's trips in this period is a swap she did for a friend.

There are three flights a day from base to Mumbai.

There is a daily flight from base to Cairo, Egypt (AB401) at 3 pm.

There is a daily flight from base to Amman, capital of Jordan.

The flight number for Base to Amman is equivalent to the Cairo flight number plus 502!

A friend asked X to do her Hyderabad trip so she could go to a wedding.

A friend asked X to do her Mumbai trip so she could visit her sick mother.

This airline flies to four destinations in India: Delhi, Mumbai, Chennai and Hyderabad.

The airline has three UK destinations: London Heathrow, London Gatwick and Manchester.

X will always swap trips to help in a medical emergency but not for a social event.

Flights to Mumbai leave at 4 am (AB504), 1.30 pm (AB502) and 10.30 pm (AB500).

Flights leave for Hyderabad at 4 am (AB570).

There are two LHR to Base flights that arrive in the morning: AB004 and AB006.

Mumbai flights are operated by the A330 aircraft.

Amman flights are operated by the A330 aircraft.

Cairo flights are operated by the A330 aircraft.

Hyderabad flights are operated by the A330 aircraft.

All London Heathrow flights are operated by the B777 aircraft except AB005/006, which are operated by the A330.

X has two A330 aircraft flights in this period.

X has one B777 aircraft flight in this period.

Managing the exercise

Distribute the clue cards randomly amongst the group. If the group provides an incorrect answer simply say, 'The solution is incorrect'. Do not give any further information even if pressed.

Answer

Monday 1st, Base to London Heathrow (003)
2nd, Heathrow to Base (004)
3rd, Rest
4th, Base to Mumbai to Base (504/505)
5th, Off
6th, Off
7th, Base to Amman to Base (903/904).

Assessment/debrief

To what degree do any of the participants raise the issue of accuracy versus speed? How does the group react if an incorrect solution is offered?

Shifting constraints

After 15 minutes change the scores to 35 for a correct solution and -40 for an incorrect solution; or after 20 minutes remove the penalty for breaking the rules.

Index

abstract reasoning   110
activities   111–30
  adding extra tasks   113–15
  amending/adapting   112–13,
    137, 141–258
  computer–based testing   128
  creativity   128
  departmentally-based tasks
    122–23
  devising from scratch
    115–16
  group   116–21, 129
    constructing   120–21
    effectiveness   118–19
  in trays   122
  performance feedback   126–27,
    141
  presentations   127–28
  role plays   121–22, 129,
    141–67
  samples   123–25

see also analytical/report
    writing, group activities, in
    trays, role plays
adverse impact   131–32
American Psychological
    Association   3
analytical/report writing   178–91
  examples   178–80, 181–82,
    183–85, 186–89, 190–91
aptitude/ability tests   87–88,
    90–91, 103
Asia Pacific Federation of Human
    Resource Management   3
assessment   64–74
  disagreements about   74
  effects of non-verbal
    information   64–65
  feedback   75–81
  future direction   128–29
  psychological biases   135–36
  ratings/scoring   71–74

recording   68–74
  coding evidence   71
  observations   69–70
  social biases   66–67
assessment centres
  acting by candidates   24–25
  activities   111–30
  benefits of   22–26
  case for   7–26, 130–31
  communicating with
      participants   55–60
  contamination of process   21
  costs   23
  cultural issues   20–21
  definition of   9–10
  designing and running   47–62,
      133–34
  effectiveness   11–13
  evaluating   60–62
  exercise effect   50–51, 65, 134
  face validity   18, 119, 126
  fairness   18–19
  further reading   130–31
  group activities   10, 52–55, 58,
      116–21, 129, 192–258
  impression on candidates   25
  legally defensible   25
  managing exercises   51
  materials   51
  relevance   22–23
  reliability   17
  sample timetable   49
  time commitment   47–48
  use of   9, 50–55

utility   19–20
validity of   14–17, 24
assessors   63–85, 134–36
  deployment   84
  interaction with participants
      67–68, 85
  recording observations
      68–74
  recruiting   81–82
  sample observation grid   85
  skills   63–74, 134–36
  training   82–83, 85
attribution theory   23, 79–81, 135
  global/specific   79
  internal   79
  stable/unstable   79
  usefulness   80–81
attitudes   132
Australian Psychological
    Society   3

behaviour, assessing   14, 16–17
  competence frameworks and
      33–35
'Big 5' personality dimensions
    88–89, 95, 98–99
British Psychological Society (BPS)
    3, 87, 95, 100–01, 137
  best practice guidelines   18–19,
      60, 130–31
  Coaching Psychology Special
      Group   134
  Psychological Testing Centre
      (PTC)   101

California Psychological
    Personality Inventory (CPI)
    88
candidates/participants   14–17
    acting   24–25
    attitudes   16, 132
    behaviour   14, 16–17, 132
    beliefs   15
    briefing   134
    communicating with   55–60
    faking   98
    feelings   15
    internal state   15
    motives   15
    personality   16
    prejudging   96
Canadian Psychological
    Association   3
categorization/stereotypes   64
Cattell, Raymond B   103
Chartered Institute of Personnel
    and Development (CPID)   3,
    19, 22, 28, 54, 95
    Recruitment, Retention and
        Turnover Survey (2006)
        9, 20, 86
coaching   85, 134–35
competence   133
competence frameworks   27–46
    cultural context   37–38
    developing   31–33, 133
        behaviour indicators   33–35
        critical incident analysis
            31–33

examples of   30–31
    organizational context   37
    problems in using   36–46
    repertory grid analysis   35–36
    types   38–39
        sample   40–45
competencies   28–29, 133
    leadership   58
    standards   36
    types of   29–30
        occupationals   29
        relationals   29–30
        universals   29
conformity pressures   66
construct validity   12, 17
content validity   12
criterion validity   12–13, 17, 90
    personality inventories   91
    sample report   93–94
critical incident analysis
    31–33

debriefing   59–60
development centres   11, 92
    debriefing and   59–60, 119
    feedback   75–81
    see also activities, assessment
development plans   75–79

emotional intelligence   132
emotional labour   24–25, 132
equal opportunities   19
European Association for
        Personnel Management   3

evaluation 60–62
  sample report 61–62
exchange tactics 66
exercise effect 50–51, 65, 134
extremity shifts 66

face validity 18, 119, 126
feedback 75–81
  written 75–77
15FQ+ personality test 103–07
Fundamental Interpersonal
  Relations Orientation-
  Behaviour (FIRO-B) 88

group activities/tasks 10, 58,
  116–21, 129, 192–258
  composition 52
  exercise constraints 52
  leading 53
  open-ended decision making
    192–214
  mental 225–44
  physical 215–24
  size 52
  supplementary activities
    245–58
    committee on anti-social
      behaviour exercise
      246–50
    flight roster 255–58
    paper castle exercise
      250–52
    word groups exercise
      252–54

'halo' effect 66
heuristics 65
Holt, Jeremy 119
Hong Kong Institute of Human
  Resource Management 3

impression management 98
International Test Commission
  (ITC) 3
  guidelines on use of
    psychometric tests 95
in tray activities 10, 122, 168–77
  examples 170–71, 172–73,
    174–77
  time management 168
interviews 10, 15–17
  competence-based 17

leadership 58

Management Standards Centre
  (MSC) 30
McHendry, Robert 128
mental task group activities
  225–44
  broadcast appeal exercise
    240–41
  cash register exercise
    228–34
  letter cards exercise 226–27
  programme planning exercise
    235–39
  who got the job exercise
    242–44